Historical American Biographies

THOMAS PAINE

Revolutionary Patriot and Writer

Pat McCarthy

Enslow Publishers, Inc.

40 Industrial Road   PO Box 38
Box 398   Aldershot
Berkeley Heights, NJ 07922   Hants GU12 6BP
USA   UK

http://www.enslow.com

To Steve Miller, for all his support and encouragement,
and to Steve Weaver, who helped me cut
nine thousand words from this book.

Copyright © 2001 by Pat McCarthy

Library of Congress Cataloging-in-Publication Data

McCarthy, Pat, 1940–
    Thomas Paine : revolutionary patriot and writer / Pat McCarthy.
        p. cm. — (Historical American biographies)
    Includes bibliographical references and index.
    ISBN 0-7660-1446-0
    1. Paine, Thomas, 1737–1809—Juvenile literature. 2. Political
scientists—United States—Biography—Juvenile literature.
3. Revolutionaries—United States—Biography—Juvenile literature.
[1. Paine, Thomas, 1737–1809. 2. Political scientists.] I. Title. II. Series.
JC178.V5 M33 2001
320.5'1'092—dc21

                               00-009261

Printed in the United States of America

10 9 8 7 6 5 4 3 2

To Our Readers: We have done our best to make sure all Internet addresses in this book were active and appropriate when we went to press. However, the author and the publisher have no control over and assume no liability for the material available on those Internet sites or on other Web sites they may link to. Any comments or suggestions can be sent by e-mail to comments@enslow.com or to the address on the back cover.

Illustration Credits: © Corel Corporation, p. 99; Enslow Publishers, Inc., pp. 7, 15, 56; Huguenot-Thomas Paine Historical Association, p. 115; John Grafton, *The American Revolution: A Picture Sourcebook* (New York: Dover Publications, Inc., 1975), pp. 10, 29, 37, 41, 49, 58, 63, 70; Library of Congress, pp. 69, 74, 84, 87; National Archives, p. 27; Reproduced from the *Dictionary of American Portraits*, Published by Dover Publications, Inc., in 1967, pp. 4, 21, 30, 32, 51; Reproduced from the *Dictionary of American Portraits*, Published by Dover Publications, Inc., in 1967, Engraved by J. B. Forrest after a painting by John Trumball, p. 47; Reproduced from the *Dictionary of American Portraits*, Published by Dover Publications, Inc., in 1967, Painting by Charles Willson Peale, Courtesy of Independence National Historic Park, p. 54; Reproduced from the *Dictionary of American Portraits*, Published by Dover Publications, Inc., in 1967, Engraving by W. G. Jackman, p. 86; Reproduced from the *Dictionary of American Portraits*, Published by Dover Publications, Inc., in 1967, Painting by Gilbert Stuart, p. 93.

Cover Illustration: Thomas Paine National Historical Association, New Rochelle, NY (Portrait); Enslow Publishers, Inc. (Background).

CONTENTS

Thomas Paine

1

INSPIRATION IN A CRISIS

It was December 1776. The American colonies were fighting to gain their independence from Great Britain. Thomas Paine had spent several months in the army, first as secretary to General Daniel Roberdau in Amboy, New Jersey, then at Fort Lee, where he had been aide-de-camp to General Nathanael Greene.

Most of the action was centered in New York and New Jersey. The British had held Staten Island, New York City, and some forts on the Hudson River since August and September 1776. This cut New York off from Pennsylvania, which would make it easy for the British to take Philadelphia, the colonial capital.

Paine served as field correspondent for the Philadelphia press. His eyewitness reports were eagerly received by the American public. He wrote while sitting around the campfire in the evenings, resting his paper on a drumhead.

Paine was headed to Philadelphia to write another pamphlet. His first pamphlet, *Common Sense*, had been published January 10, 1776. It had helped convince the American people to declare their independence from Great Britain. It sold 150,000 copies and was actually the first American best-seller. He tried to make people understand the dangers of the moment without discouraging them.

In November, British troops, along with hired German soldiers called Hessians, made a surprise attack on Fort Lee, New Jersey, forcing General Greene's army to retreat to Trenton, New Jersey. Paine stood across the river from Fort Washington with General Greene, sadly watching the British takeover. The men were unable to do a thing to stop Charles Cornwallis, the British general.[1]

The situation was critical for the Americans. On December 1, the volunteers from New Jersey and Maryland would complete their one-year term of enlistment. Expected reinforcements had not arrived.

The cold, hungry, and sick American troops slogged along the muddy roads to Trenton. Morale was low, and General George Washington himself was discouraged. This untrained, shabbily dressed army had little chance against the highly trained and warmly dressed British Redcoats. Washington was fighting against great odds. He wrote to a relative, "Your imagination can scarce extend to a situation more distressing than mine. Our only dependence now is upon the

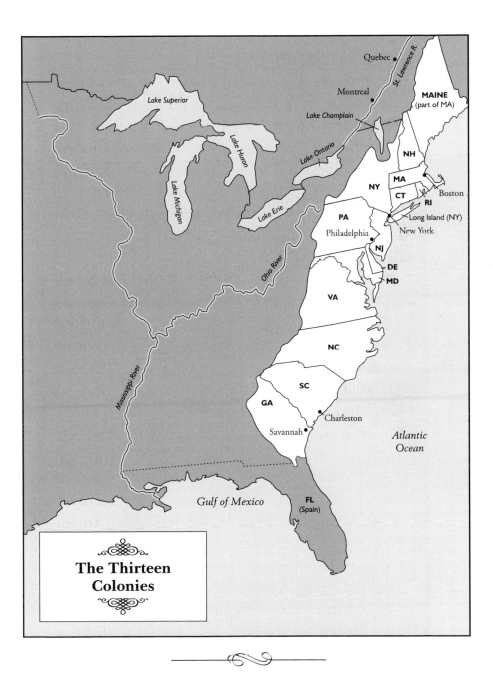

The Thirteen Colonies

As more American cities came under British attack, many worried that Philadelphia would be taken next.

speedy enlistment of a new army. If this fails, I think the game will be pretty well up. . . ."[2]

As Thomas Paine neared Philadelphia, refugees streamed out of the city, wagons piled high with their belongings. People were sure Philadelphia would soon fall to the British. Even the Second Continental Congress, a group of representatives from all the colonies who met to coordinate their efforts in dealing with Great Britain, had withdrawn to Baltimore.

Angered by what he saw and the attitude of the people, Paine got out his notes and quickly wrote a pamphlet that would have great influence on the American war effort. In what he called "a passion of patriotism," Paine wrote the first of his *Crisis* papers. He said he wrote "in a rage when our affairs were at their lowest ebb and things in a most gloomy state."[3] While others criticized General Washington for retreating, Paine praised him, insisting that safe retreat on the battlefield is the most difficult art to perfect.

Paine boasted of the strength the regrouping American troops would have: "Our new army at both ends of the continent is recruiting fast, and we shall be able to open the next campaign with 60,000 men, well armed and clothed."[4] This was probably an exaggeration, but he knew it was important for people to support Washington and his troops. He called the British offensive war "unjustified murder." According to Paine, America's defensive war was necessary to protect her people and their property.[5]

Paine entitled the eight-page-long pamphlet *The American Crisis I*. He knew other crises would come and he would write about them, too. Eighteen thousand copies were printed the week before Christmas.

By December 23, copies of Paine's first pamphlet had reached army headquarters. General Washington was greatly impressed with Paine's work. In the late afternoon on Christmas Day, by the light of their lanterns, his officers read it aloud to their squads.[6]

Washington's five thousand troops were freezing and lacked warm clothes. Some even had no shoes. The weather worsened and the anticipated recruits failed to arrive.

Washington had decided that Christmas night would be the ideal time to attack the British. Most of the British troops were German Hessians. The general knew the Germans made a great celebration of Christmas, and he hoped the festivities would distract the soldiers. The bad weather also helped. Visibility was greatly limited by fog and sleet.

When darkness fell, Washington moved his troops across the Delaware River from Pennsylvania to New Jersey. Sleet pelted down as the flat-bottomed boats made their way across the river.

Opening Lines of *The American Crisis I*

These are the times that try men's souls. The summer soldier and the sunshine patriot will, in this crisis, shrink from the service of their country. . . . Tyranny, like hell, is not easily conquered.[7]

The image of George Washington crossing the Delaware River with his troops has become one of the most famous of the American Revolution.

Washington's attack worked brilliantly. The British and Hessians were taken completely by surprise. After heavy fighting, the Americans captured a thousand prisoners as well as all the enemy stores, including fine German swords.

The success of Washington's plan was partly due to surprise and the weather, but some credit has to be given to Thomas Paine. A soldier's morale has a great deal to do with his performance in combat. Paine's stirring words brought hope and inspiration to the American soldiers. The victory at Trenton put the Americans back into the war and did much to revive the flagging spirits of the soldiers.

2

GROWING UP IN THETFORD

Thomas Paine was born on January 29, 1737, in a cottage on Bridge Street in Thetford, a little village in Norfolk County, England. His parents were Joseph and Frances Cocke Pain (Thomas changed the spelling when he went to America). Joseph was a staymaker who made women's corsets (tight-fitting undergarments). Staymakers were in the same social class as other craftsmen. Frances Cocke, on the other hand, was from a family of a higher social class. Her father was a prominent lawyer. He opposed her marriage to Pain because of the difference in their ages. Joseph was twenty-six and Frances thirty-seven when they married on June 20, 1734. Her father's disapproval, however, may also have been because Frances was marrying beneath her.

Religious Differences

Joseph Pain and Frances Cocke also practiced different religions, which caused even more conflict. She was a member of the Anglican Church, the official church of England. It later became the Episcopalian Church in the United States. Joseph's church, the Quakers, was not recognized by the state.

Quakers believed that all people were equal before God. Quakers tried to improve the lives of the poor, the oppressed, and the enslaved. They also believed that an inner spiritual light from God inspired them to do good.

Most of the population looked down on the Quakers, officially known as the Society of Friends. The Toleration Act of 1689 gave them the right to practice their religion, but they were not allowed to vote or hold public office, and they could not enroll in the public universities at Oxford and Cambridge.

Frances Pain was said to have a "sour temper and eccentric character." Joseph, on the other hand, was a meek and mild man.[1] Tom grew up an only child. His younger sister died in infancy.

Tom was baptized in the Anglican Church, but his father's Quaker beliefs influenced him more. He always stood up for the underdog and worked to improve conditions for those who had little. But the conflict between his parents' faiths took its toll on the child.

When he was a small boy, Tom first heard about the crucifixion of Jesus Christ. Years later, in his book, *Age of Reason*, he recalled the horror he had felt:

I well remember, when about seven or eight years of
age, hearing a sermon read by a relation of mine, . . .
upon the subject of what is called Redemption by the
death of the Son of God. . . . I revolted at the
recollection of what I had heard, and I thought to
myself that it was making Almighty God act like a
passionate man that he killed his son. . . . I believed
that God was too good to do such an action. . . . I
believe in the same manner to this moment: And I
moreover believe that any system of religion that has
anything in it that shocks the mind of a child cannot
be a true system.[2]

So Tom rejected Christianity at an early age, and
remarks such as these later caused many to consider
him an atheist (one who does not believe in God).
However, this was not true. As he stated on many
occasions, he did believe in God. For most of his life,
Tom considered himself a Quaker, though he did not
entirely agree with their beliefs, either.

Life in Thetford

Thetford was a village of two thousand people on the
main road to London. It was dirty and smelled bad, as
did most villages of the time, because it had no sewage
system. Rows of houses attached to one another lined
the streets. There was no running water. People got
water from wells in the streets. Lanterns holding can-
dles lit the street corners at night.

There was not much entertainment in Thetford.
Middle-class ladies enjoyed picnics and teas. Most
of the men liked gambling, drinking, and cockfighting,
a sport that pitted two roosters against each other,

fighting until one died. Occasionally, there was a dance at an inn or tavern.

The Pains' thatched cottage was near Gallows Hill, where many convicted criminals were hanged. The Quaker meetinghouse, which held fifty people, was next door to the jail. Tom sympathized with the condemned, who had often done nothing worse than steal a bit of food for their starving families. Those who were not hanged were branded, whipped publicly, or fined and put in prison.

The duke of Grafton controlled Thetford. The town was known as a "pocket borough," which meant that the duke had the people's votes "in his pocket." Because of his power, they all voted the way he told them to.

School Days

Many children started working or serving as apprentices when they were only five or six years old. An apprentice worked for at least seven years for a craftsman to learn a trade. Craftsmen included weavers, tanners, carpenters, farriers (blacksmiths), masons, and bakers. Children sometimes worked as many as twelve hours a day.

The Pains did not want this kind of life for their son. When he was seven, they sent him to the village school. He learned to read and write, but his father would not allow him to learn Latin. Quakers objected to the pagan (non-Christian) philosophies of the Roman writers.

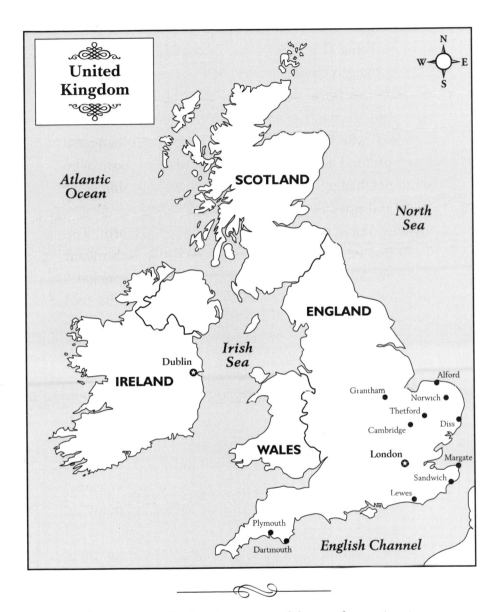

United Kingdom

Atlantic
Ocean

SCOTLAND

North
Sea

ENGLAND

Irish
Sea

Dublin

IRELAND

Alford

Grantham

Norwich

Thetford

Cambridge

Diss

WALES

London

Margate

Sandwich

Lewes

Plymouth

Dartmouth

English Channel

Thomas Paine, who later became one of the most famous American patriots, was born in a small town in England.

Tom was good at math and science. "The natural bent of my mind was to science," he wrote. "I had some turn, and I believe some talent, for poetry."[3] Others said his verse was just bad poetry.

Tom's curiosity and intelligence caused his teacher, Reverend William Knowles, to take an interest in him. Knowles told the boy stories of his adventures at sea and loaned him books. One, *A Natural History of Virginia*, sparked Tom's interest in visiting the New World. He later said, "My inclination from that day for seeing the western side of the Atlantic never left me."[4]

Years later, a writer went to Thetford to find out about Thomas Paine's early life. He was told that Tom had been "a sharp boy of unsettled application; . . . who left no performances which denote a juvenile vigor of uncommon attainments."[5] The people of Thetford showed no pride in Tom's accomplishments while he was alive.

Thomas Paine, Poet
When Tom was eight, his pet crow died. He wrote this poem and recited it when he buried the bird in the backyard.

> Here lies the body of John Crow,
> Who once was high but now is low:
> Ye brother Crows take warning all,
> For as you rise, so must you fall.[6]

Apprentice

When Tom was thirteen, his parents took him out of school to work as an apprentice in his father's stay-maker's shop. Tom did not like anything about the job. He thought corset-making should be women's work. Furthermore, his father's business was falling off, and he would not be able to take Tom into partnership. When he was nineteen and his apprenticeship ended, Tom Paine ran away. Remembering his teacher's tales of life at sea, he signed on as a hand aboard a privateer, the *Terrible*. Privateers were privately owned ships that were licensed by the government to attack enemy merchant ships and seize their cargo.

France was Great Britain's enemy at the time, so French ships were a frequent target of privateers. The two countries were engaged in the Seven Years' War, which was called the French and Indian War in the American colonies. The war was fought both on the sea and in America.

When a privateer captured a merchant ship, the cargo was divided among the captain, officers, and crew. Most men were in it for the money, not because of any sense of patriotism.

Tom thought this would be an exciting life. He was eager to sail with Captain William Death on the *Terrible*. When Joseph Pain learned what Tom had done, he hurried to the ship and convinced him not to go.[7]

Tom soon read in the newspaper that the *Terrible* had been in a bloody battle with a French privateer.

One hundred fifty members of its crew had died, including the captain and all but one of the officers. Tom had had a lucky escape.

Thomas Paine then found a job as a journeyman, or assistant, staymaker in London, working for master staymaker John Morris. The money he made paid the rent on a small, shabby room.

He was amazed by the noise, violence, and robbery in London. Crowds of beggars, swarms of dogs, and cattle being driven through the streets added to the chaos. He hated the long hours and the boring job.[8]

Running Away to a Life at Sea

On January 17, 1757, just after his twentieth birthday, Thomas Paine signed onto another privateer, the *King of Prussia*. This time, his father did not stop him. Thomas Paine never discussed his experiences at sea in his later writings.

While he was on board, the *King of Prussia* captured and plundered several enemy ships. It also rescued a friendly ship that had been attacked by a French privateer. The *King of Prussia* docked at Dartmouth, England, on August 20, 1757. There is no record of its sailing again. Paine's share of the booty has been estimated at about thirty pounds, a substantial sum for someone brought up in relative poverty. He decided not to go to sea again, but to stay in London and enjoy life there.

3

TWO JOBS AND A MARRIAGE

Six months later, when the money Paine had made at sea ran out, he found a position with a stay-maker in County Kent. In the spring of 1758, he began working with Benjamin Grace, a master staymaker. Paine, however, was not satisfied with the job.

The next spring, with the help of a ten-pound (British currency) loan from Grace, Tom Paine set up his own shop in the town of Sandwich, about seventy-five miles southeast of London. A seventeenth-century cottage served as both home and place of business to Paine. Today, one can see a small plaque at the build-ing that reads, "Tom Paine's cottage c. 1759. Author of Rights of Man. Inspired the American Declaration of Independence."[1]

When he was not working in the shop, Paine sometimes preached. According to the journal of John Wesley, founder of the Methodist Church, Benjamin Grace had taken Paine to the Methodist Chapel in Dover and Paine became a member.[2]

The Methodist Church taught people self-respect, self-government, self-reliance, and organizational skills. It helped the poor with food and clothing. It also taught that God's grace shines equally on the rich and the poor, and that God welcomes everybody. These beliefs appealed to Paine. He always had compassion for the poor. He was impressed to find a religion that not only included them, but also accepted them as equals.

Marriage

In the summer of 1759, Paine met Mary Lambert, who was referred to as "a pretty girl of modest behavior."[3] Mary's parents had died, and she worked as a personal maid to Maria Solly, wife of prominent businessman Richard Solly. Nothing is known of their courtship, but the young couple married at St. Peter's Church in Sandwich on September 27, 1759.

A few months later, Paine's business failed, probably due to his poor business sense. He and Mary moved ten miles up the coast to Margate, a fishing town known for its fresh sea air and cold bathing. Mary was pregnant, so they may have moved there for her health. It has been said that Paine had to leave Sandwich one night to avoid his creditors, taking only Mary, his tools, and a few belongings. Whatever the

John Wesley was the founder of Methodism, a religion that appealed to Thomas Paine.

reason for the move, it did not help Mary. She died a few months later in childbirth. The baby also died. Paine was left alone at age twenty-three, with no wife and no job.

Customs Officer

Mary's father, James Lambert, had been a customs officer for the British tax department. Paine decided that being a customs officer might be a good job for him. Joseph Pain agreed, so Paine spent the next year living with his parents and studying for the required examinations.

The job involved collecting a tax charged mainly on alcoholic beverages, but also on salt, soap, tobacco, and other goods. The customs officer had to measure the brewers' casks to see how much they held, and write reports to send to London. Most people in England hated the tax officers because the taxes were extremely high. One quart of liquor had a tax equal to the weekly wage of the poorest laborers. There was a lot of smuggling along the coast, and tax officers were expected to stop the smugglers, in addition to collecting taxes. Being a tax officer was a dangerous business. For all this, an officer was paid fifty pounds a year. Out of that sum, he needed to take care of the horse that he rode on his rounds.

Paine had to get a birth certificate and letters of recommendation from local people. He also had to swear an oath that he had not bribed anyone to get the job. In the fall of 1761, a local supervisor visited to check his health, personal habits, intelligence, and handwriting ability. Next, a local tax man taught him to measure the various sizes and shapes of kegs and write down the measurements. Finally, he took a formal examination, which determined whether he could write clear English and do arithmetic. Another test showed his skill at measuring casks, writing the records in a notebook, and issuing receipts and invoices.

In December 1762, fourteen months after he first applied for the job, Paine received a position at Grantham, in Lincolnshire. His job was measuring brewers' casks. In August 1764, he was promoted to a better-paying job in Alford, a small market town near the North Sea coast. There, he was required to collect revenues from coffee and tea dealers and watch for smugglers.

At Alford, Paine made his rounds on horseback, often over muddy roads that became impassable when it rained. He carried his measuring stick, covered with figures, and an ink bottle slung from his buttonhole. He also patrolled the coast on horseback, watching for smugglers. Luckily, he did not have any run-ins with these potentially dangerous men.

Because they did not want to irritate the already hostile merchants, many tax men fell into the habit of merely accepting whatever the owner told them the goods were worth. They did not bother to measure the casks, but applied the tax stamp without inspecting the goods. This was known as stamping. It happened partly because tax officers had to work long rounds for poor pay, and partly because of the attitude of the business owners.

Paine may have fallen into this practice. He was discharged from the tax service about a year after he started his job in Alford. There was a rumor that he had written a letter confessing his guilt. However, there is no record of the confession. At any rate, Tom Paine was again left without a job. Twenty-eight years old and penniless, he was forced to go home to Thetford.

4

DISILLUSIONED WITH ENGLAND

After he lost the tax job, Paine worked as a journeyman staymaker in Diss, a small dismal town about fifteen miles from Thetford. After a short stint at Diss, Paine decided to return to London. He was bored with staymaking and often quarreled about religion with his boss, Mr. Gudgeon, and fellow journeymen.[1]

Paine got a job teaching English in an academy for the children of artisans, or local craftsmen. Such small schools gave children from working-class backgrounds a chance to learn such skills as arithmetic, writing business letters, technical drawing, and bookkeeping.

Paine enjoyed the intellectual stimulation he found in London. He renewed relations with the scientists in the Royal Society. He had become acquainted with them in the months after he served on the *King of Prussia*. He also met Dr. John Bevis, a leading astronomer and an expert on earthquakes.

Paine learned more about the Methodist Church and was impressed by the Methodists' concern for the poor and social justice. Some say he preached to people in open fields in the city.

Tax Man Again

In the summer of 1767, Paine applied for reinstatement in the tax service. His letter was humble in tone. He admitted the grave error of judgment that had led to his dismissal. He thanked the tax board for being lenient, but denied that he had ever been dishonest.[2]

In February 1768, the tax board offered him a position in Lewes in Sussex, a bustling market town about twice the size of Thetford and much more lively. Lewes boasted a busy coffeehouse, a theater group, a library, and a cricket team. Cricket is an English game somewhat similar to baseball.

Paine found lodging in the large house of former town constable Samuel Ollive and his family. The shop, a kitchen, and a sitting room were downstairs, with two stories of bedrooms above. Paine's large room overlooked the street.

With his wife, Esther, and daughter, Elizabeth, Ollive ran a snuff and tobacco shop. Chewing snuff, a smokeless tobacco, was a popular practice. But business was slow, so Paine's rent money helped pay the bills. Ollive had formerly been part owner of the White Hart Inn.[3] The White Hart became a second home to

Paine. He also became very active in the Headstrong Club, a "voluntary association of public-spirited Lewes citizens who met once a week to debate pressing local, national, and international matters."[4] The men probably debated government corruption, injustice, reforms, and the issue of whether there should be a king. Paine was a dominant personality in the inner circle at the inn.

Paine always loved conversation, and found total acceptance there. He met people like William Lee, owner of the *Sussex Weekly Advertiser* and *Lewes Journal*, and Thomas "Clio" Rickman, who became a close friend. Lee said Paine was "a shrewd and sensible fellow" who enjoyed an unusual "depth of political knowledge."[5] Clio Rickman, a young poet and printer, became Paine's lifelong friend and one of his first biographers. He described Paine as "notorious for that quality which has been defined as perseverance in a good cause and obstinacy in a bad one."[6]

When there was a debate in the Headstrong Club, the winner received what was called the Headstrong Book. The winner could keep it until the next week's debate. Paine often won the prize.

He began writing poetry, including an elegy (a poem of praise for the dead) on the death of General James Wolfe, who had been killed in the Battle of Quebec during the French and Indian War. He also wrote a long humorous poem called "Farmer Short's Dog Porter: A Tale."

Thomas Paine, with his intelligence and wit, became a popular member of intellectual circles.

Another Marriage and a New Task

In July 1769, Samuel Ollive died. Thinking there could be gossip about his living in the same house with a widow, Paine moved out of the Ollives' home. Esther and Elizabeth Ollive tried to run the snuff shop alone, but soon asked Paine to help. They expanded the store to carry groceries as well as tobacco and snuff. Still, it went steadily downhill.

The intelligent and pretty Elizabeth ran a boarding school for young ladies. On March 26, 1771, twelve years after the death of his first wife, Thomas Paine married Elizabeth Ollive in Westgate Chapel.

The year after his marriage, Paine was asked by his fellow tax officers to write a pamphlet presenting their case for a pay raise to Parliament (the British legislature). A petition was drawn up and circulated among the officers. Each man contributed three shillings to cover Paine's expenses in London. These included the cost of printing the pamphlet and food and lodging.

This was Paine's first formal piece of writing. The pamphlet, *Case of the Officers of Excise*, was clearly written and showed the same logic and persuasiveness as his later works. Paine wrote a brief introduction, then divided his arguments into three sections. The first considered the low salary of the excise worker. A tax officer made only fifty pounds a year, and it cost fourteen pounds to care for the horse he needed for the job. A common laborer made as much. The second section discussed the fact that poverty causes corruption and dishonesty. The third restated his purpose and saw a revised service in which the officers would receive a higher wage.

With the five hundred pounds raised by his fellow officers, Paine had four thousand copies of the pamphlet printed. He spent the winter of 1772–1773 in London, talking to members of Parliament and other influential people.

Paine had no success convincing Parliament, however. The legislators rejected the petition immediately. England was often at war and needed money to pay its debts. Paine thought King George III himself caused the petition to fail. Paine was quoted as saying, "The King, or somebody for him, applied to Parliament to have his own salary raised a hundred thousand pounds a year."[7]

Paine Loses Everything

Disappointed, Paine returned to Lewes. His whole life seemed to be falling apart. On April 14 and 15, 1773, his belongings were sold at auction to pay his debts.

High officials in the excise service were angered by his pamphlet, but because the law gave Englishmen the right to petition, they could not fire him. However, the officials charged that he had taken several months off without leave to go to London, which he had.[8]

In June, he and his wife, Elizabeth, signed a legal separation document. They never saw each other again. Much gossip and controversy accompanied the separation. Neither Paine nor his wife would ever discuss the separation. Paine told his friend and biographer, Clio Rickman, "It is nobody's business by my own; I had cause for it, but I will name it to no one."[9] When another friend questioned him about it, Paine replied, "I never answer impertinent [rude] questions."[10] In his biography of Paine, Clio Rickman wrote, "Mr. Paine always spoke tenderly and respectfully of his wife." He also said that Paine anonymously sent her small sums of money over the years.[11]

Paine developed a dislike for King George III, seen here, even while still living in England. Paine would later come to view the king as a strong political enemy during the American Revolution.

Benjamin Franklin helped Paine get his start in America by giving him a letter of introduction to prominent American colonists.

Thirty-seven-year-old Paine returned to London with no money, no job, and no family. He did not stay there long. With the encouragement of Benjamin Franklin, a well-known American colonist, whom he had met through his old friend and lecturer James Ferguson, Paine decided to try his luck in the New World. Carrying a letter of introduction from Franklin, he boarded the ship *London Packet* in September 1774. At last, he was on his way to see the New World he had read about in his schoolmaster's books.

5

COMMON SENSE

It was said that Thomas Paine had received money from his wife in their separation agreement, which enabled him to book a first-class berth on the *London Packet*.[1] Despite this bit of luxury, Paine contracted typhus during the voyage and suffered from a high fever, pains, and a rash. Almost everyone on board was affected. Five passengers died. Paine nearly gave up hope of ever seeing America.

When the ship docked in Philadelphia on November 30, Paine was still too ill to turn over in bed. A Philadelphia doctor, John Kearsley, heard that Paine had a letter of introduction from Benjamin Franklin. He had Paine carried off the ship on a stretcher and taken to the home of John Keen, where Kearsley tended him for six weeks.

Writer and Editor in America

While still confined to the house, Paine wrote an essay entitled *Dialogue Between General Wolfe and General Gage in a Wood near Boston*. This was an imaginary conversation between the British governor of Massachusetts and a general who had been killed in the Battle of Quebec. It appeared in a local newspaper on January 4, 1775, and established Paine as a writer in his new homeland.

When he was finally able to go out, Paine visited Richard Bache, the husband of Benjamin Franklin's only daughter, Sarah. Bache was a well-to-do marine insurance underwriter who later became postmaster general of the United States. He found Paine a job tutoring the sons of several friends.

Paine found a place to stay on Market Street, in the heart of the city. He lived near the auction shed of

the Philadelphia slave market, which may have given him a firsthand look at the buying and selling of African slaves.

Paine enjoyed visiting the London Coffeehouse and the Indian Queen

One of Paine's earliest friends in America was Sarah Bache, the only daughter of Benjamin Franklin.

Hotel, where most of the political leaders of the area met. He soon came to know the men who would be the leaders of the new nation.

Philadelphia, with a population of thirty-five thousand, was the largest and wealthiest city in the colonies. Unlike older English towns, it was cheerful and attractive. It had shade trees, gardens, and spacious cobbled streets lined with red brick houses and white church spires.

Paine browsed in the bookshops. His favorite, run by Robert Aitken, was just around the corner from his room. Aitken's shop had one of the largest collection of books in the colonies. Aitken soon noticed the tall slim newcomer with his gray-streaked brown hair pulled back in a short ponytail. He talked to him one morning and was impressed with Paine's energy and knowledge of books and politics.[2]

Dissatisfaction With the British Government

At that time, the colonies were growing dissatisfied with the British Parliament and the taxes it was imposing on the people living in the colonies. It seemed to them that Great Britain was using the colonies to pay for its recent war with France by passing the Sugar Act, the Stamp Act, the Townshend Acts, and the Tea Act, all of which charged taxes for items colonists used every day.

Although most considered themselves English, many of the colonists thought the British government should not have a right to tax them. They reasoned that they should not be taxed because they had no direct representatives in Parliament who could vote on whether the colonists agreed with the tax. American colonists thought it was unfair to tax people who had no direct say in their government. This prompted the saying, "Taxation without representation is tyranny."

Philadelphia was the best place for Thomas Paine to learn about the political climate in the colonies. The First Continental Congress had ended recently, and the second was set to gather in May 1775. These were meetings of representatives from all the American colonies. Its members tried to decide what the colonies should do about their problems with Great Britain. Paine took great interest as each event brought the colonies closer to a showdown with the king.

Bookstore owner Robert Aitken asked Paine to edit a new periodical. The monthly, called *Pennsylvania Magazine*, was to be a uniquely American magazine. It would be for the American colonies about the American colonies. Paine took the job in February 1775. He wrote much of the content of the magazine.

The magazine prospered. In three months, it increased its circulation from six hundred to fifteen hundred. Paine wrote articles under various pen names.

At first, Paine thought the conflict between Great Britain and the colonies would be settled peacefully. He later recalled, "I supposed the parties would find a way either to decide or settle it. I had no thoughts of independence or arms. The world could not have persuaded me that I should be either a soldier or author."[3]

Pennsylvania Magazine
The first issue of *Pennsylvania Magazine* consisted of fifty-two pages stitched together between blue paper covers. It included a character sketch of Voltaire (a French writer and philosopher), a report on American beavers, an essay on suicides, and cures for "putrid fevers." There was also a puzzle called "A Mathematical Question Proposed," which Paine probably wrote.[4]

In March 1775, Paine wrote an article denouncing African slavery. With his Quaker background, he was opposed to the enslavement of human beings. He asked the colonists "with what consistency, or decency they complain so loudly of attempts to enslave them, while they hold so many hundred thousands in slavery, and annually enslave many thousands more, without any pretense of authority or claim over them?"[5]

Revolution Breaks Out

Paine's attention was soon taken away from the slavery issue. On April 25, 1775, an exhausted rider leaped from his horse at the City Tavern in Philadelphia. He brought shocking news. He told of a bloody skirmish that had recently taken place between American militiamen and British troops at Lexington, Massachusetts.

On April 19, 1775, an army of twelve hundred British troops led by Lord Hugh Percy had marched out of Boston, accompanied by drums and fifes. They were on their way to seize the supply dump where colonists kept their ammunition at Concord, near Boston. Three Boston patriots on horseback—Paul Revere, William Dawes, and Samuel Prescott—had spread the word that the British were coming. The minutemen—colonial troops who claimed they would be ready to fight at a minute's notice—were prepared.

Percy found the minutemen waiting at Lexington, and his men fired at them. Eight Americans fell immediately, and the ensuing battle raged for twelve hours. The British then moved on to Concord, where they were also met in battle by American troops. The British finally retreated to Boston, carrying 273 dead and wounded. The war for American independence from Great Britain had begun.

Early in spring 1775, King George III had demanded total submission from the colonies. He expected them to follow his orders without question. General Thomas Gage, the British general sent to control the colonies, asked for twenty thousand more troops. He was told he could have half that many when weather conditions improved.

In January, Lord John Sandwich, a member of Parliament, had told the House of Lords that the American colonists "are raw, undisciplined, cowardly men. Believe me my Lords, the sound of a cannon would carry them off as fast as their feet could carry them."[6]

The Battle of Lexington was the first of the American Revolution.
After the first shots were fired, it soon became clear that the dispute
between Great Britain and the colonies could be a long one.

Sandwich did not know that the colonies had been preparing for war for several months. In Massachusetts, Connecticut, and Rhode Island, American militia troops drilled on the village greens. A force of fifteen thousand men led by Colonel Israel Putnam had assaulted the royal fortress at Portsmouth and carried off its cannon and supplies. The Continental Congress had voted to raise an army of eighteen thousand men.

Congress had also authorized a colonial navy and was trying to make alliances in Europe. Certain leaders, including Benjamin Franklin, Samuel Adams, and

George Washington, had come to see that independence
was necessary. However, a majority of the colonists did
not agree. Most wealthy men in the colonies had strong
ties to England.

The Quakers of Philadelphia published a paper
declaring their loyalty to the king. Paine wrote, "I am
thus far a Quaker, that I would gladly agree with all
the world to lay aside the use of arms, and settle matters by negotiation; but unless the whole world wills,
the matter ends, and I take up my musket, and thank
heaven he has put it in my power."[7]

In early May 1775, the Second Continental
Congress met. Benjamin Franklin had returned from
England, after a failed last effort at conciliation with
the king. On May 9, the delegation from New England
rode into town, to be greeted solemnly by the tolling
of muffled church bells to show sympathy for the
attacks at Lexington and Concord.

The delegates chose "the modest and virtuous, the
amiable, generous, and brave George Washington,
esquire, to be general of the American army, and that
he is to repair, as soon as possible to the camp before
Boston."[8]

The Battles of Lexington and Concord convinced
Thomas Paine that independence was the only choice.
He later wrote, "No man was a warmer wisher for
reconciliation than myself, before the fatal nineteenth
of April 1775, but the moment the event of that day
was made known, I rejected the hardened, sullen-
tempered Pharaoh of England [King George III]
forever."[9] He also said, "When the country, into which

I had just set my foot, was on fire about my ears, it was time to stir."[10]

Common Sense

Paine resigned from the *Pennsylvania Magazine* in August 1775. He began to write a pamphlet setting forth the cause for independence. In early December, the manuscript was finished. Famous physician and patriot Benjamin Rush suggested that Paine show it to Samuel Adams, the patriot from Massachusetts, and David Rittenhouse, a famous astronomer, as well as Benjamin Franklin. Paine's clear thinking, picturesque writing, and use of simple language made the tract easy for anyone to read. He had planned to call the pamphlet *Plain Truth*, but Rush persuaded him to change the title to *Common Sense*.

The first part of *Common Sense* was an attack on the English system of government. Paine labeled it corrupt, despotic (tyrannical), and contemptible (hateful). Next, Paine developed the argument that it would be foolish even to try to reconcile with such a government. The third section stated that America should be and could become an independent republic.

Scotsman Robert Bell agreed to print the pamphlet. He and Paine would split the profits. Paine promised to pay for any losses that might occur. Paine's share of the profits would go to a fund to buy mittens for American soldiers.

Bell had a thousand copies of the pamphlet ready on January 10, 1776. The first edition sold out within

two weeks, at two shillings (about a dime) a copy. Several printers reprinted the pamphlet.

Common Sense was merely signed "Author." At first, some people thought Benjamin Franklin or Benjamin Rush had written it. However, Paine made no secret of the fact that he wrote it, and it soon became common knowledge. He picked up the nickname "Common Sense." It would stick with him throughout his life.

A few days before *Common Sense* came out, Lord John Murray Dunmore had launched a sea attack on Norfolk, Virginia, leaving the city a smoldering ruin. At the end of the month, George Washington wrote from his army headquarters near Boston, "A few more of such flaming arguments as were exhibited at Falmouth and Norfolk, added to the sound doctrine and unanswerable reasoning contained in the pamphlet *Common Sense* will not leave members at a loss to decide upon the propriety of separation."[11]

Paine glowed with pride at the success of his work. Enthusiasm for the pamphlet spread through the colonies and to other countries. It actually sold more copies in France than in America.

John Adams, who would later serve as the first vice president, was not as impressed with *Common Sense*. He thought Paine's idea of a legislature with only one house was dangerous. However, he did admit he could not have written anything in "so manly and striking a style."[12]

The British press reported that American army officers were reading the pamphlet to their soldiers.

Thomas Paine's Common Sense *helped encourage the American people to support the Declaration of Independence.*

One officer said that the arrival of *Common Sense* was worth as much as five thousand men to the patriot cause.[13]

Thomas Jefferson, a member of the Continental Congress, reported to Paine that the Virginia Convention, a group of representatives from that colony meeting at Williamsburg, had voted unanimously that Virginia's delegates to the Continental Congress should propose independence.[14] Apparently, *Common Sense* had helped convince them that independence was necessary.

On Thursday, July 4, 1776, the Declaration of Independence, drafted by Jefferson, which stated that the colonies no longer belonged to Great Britain, but were an independent country, was read and approved by the Continental Congress. Thomas Paine's writing had helped cause the leaders of thirteen separate colonies to come together and fight for a common cause—independence from Great Britain.

6

CRISIS PAPERS AND SILAS DEANE

On Christmas Day, 1776, General George Washington's troops defeated the Hessians at Trenton. Three weeks later, the second paper in Paine's *Crisis* series appeared.

In this pamphlet, Thomas Paine was the first person to call the new country "The United States of America." He had helped convince the Continental Congress to declare the colonies' independence from England, creating a new country. Now he had helped give that country a name.[1]

More Problems Arise

Crisis II was an open letter to Lord Richard Howe, brother of the British commander. He had come to America to command the British Navy. He would also offer a pardon to all colonists willing to quit fighting

against the mother country. Paine said his purpose was to "expose the folly of your [Howe's] pretended authority as a commissioner; the wickedness of your cause in general; and the impossibility of your conquering us at any rate."[2]

That same month, Paine was hired as secretary to a delegation meeting with a group of Iroquois Indians at Easton, Pennsylvania, about fifty miles north of Philadelphia. The Iroquois wanted to know what their status would be under the new American government. In the few weeks it took to sign a peace treaty with the Iroquois, a state constitution was written for Pennsylvania. When Paine returned to Philadelphia, a huge political fight was taking place. The constitution favored craftsmen and back-country farmers, because it no longer required people to own property in order to vote. Wealthy colonists did not like the change.

Paine told Pennsylvanians that they needed to put aside their differences until the war was over. He helped organize the Whig Society, a group that encouraged everyone to work together for the American cause.

A New Job and More *Crisis* Papers

The Continental Congress returned to Philadelphia after the Continental Army defeated the British at Trenton and Princeton. On April 17, Congress voted to set up a committee for foreign affairs and appointed Thomas Paine secretary of the committee.

Paine, who had just turned forty, was thrilled with the appointment.[3] His job consisted of keeping records of the meetings of the committee and sending letters to foreign agents, including Benjamin Franklin, the American representative in Paris.

On April 19, 1777, the second anniversary of the Battle of Lexington, Paine's *Crisis III* was published. This pamphlet was addressed to the Quakers. In it, Paine attacked the Loyalists, people who sided with the British against the colonists. He said that anyone who refused to fight should pay high taxes, and the money should be used for the army. He thought every colonist should swear an oath of allegiance to the United States.

By the end of August, British troops were headed for Philadelphia, the American capital. Washington's army marched out to meet them. On September 11, the British Army, led by General Charles Cornwallis, sneaked in behind the colonial army and caught it by surprise at Brandywine Creek. Cornwallis's seventy-five hundred men killed or wounded a thousand American soldiers, and took four hundred others prisoner. Washington ordered a hasty retreat.

Paine believed it was only a matter of time before the British Army marched on Philadelphia. He urged the colonists to defend the city, but no one would listen. The Continental Congress fled to the town of York, ninety miles west.

Paine worked through the night writing *Crisis IV*, then rushed it to a printer. This was the shortest *Crisis* paper—only four pages. He tried to bolster the spirits of the soldiers and civilians, arguing that the British were cut off from supplies and were losing men. They

would soon be "in a condition to be afterwards totally defeated."[4] He concluded with a plea to citizens to give their full support to the army.

The Future Looks Dark

Paine loaded his belongings and the papers of the committee for foreign affairs into a boat sailing for Trenton. He would spend the next eight months wandering the back roads, avoiding British troops, and helping with the colonial military campaign. He again served as aide-de-camp to General Nathanael Greene, as he had the previous fall.

In early October, it took him three days to find Washington's troops. He was afraid to ask questions of strangers for fear they might be British sympathizers. He arrived just in time to witness the Battle of Germantown, which was being fought five miles from Philadelphia. The troops fought in a dense fog, making it difficult to tell whether they were attacking friends or enemies. The American troops were forced to retreat.

On October 17, the Americans won a decisive battle. They trapped British General John Burgoyne at Saratoga, New York, on the Hudson River north of Albany. Burgoyne had planned to cut off New England from the rest of the colonies, but instead he was forced to surrender. The colonists lost many men, but the victory boosted their morale. It also helped persuade France to ally with the young United States.

Paine spent the first two weeks of November with his friends, Joseph and Mary Kirkbride, near Bordentown, New Jersey. Then he joined a scouting

Toward the beginning of the American Revolution, Thomas Paine served as an aide to General Nathanael Greene, seen here.

party commanded by General Greene. They spent four days and nights near the mouth of the Schuylkill River, trying to find out British plans.

On November 16, Fort Mifflin on the Delaware River fell to the British, after a week-long attack. The Americans abandoned nearby Fort Mercer and burned most of their ships to keep the British from capturing them.

George Washington marched his men to Valley Forge, twenty miles up the river from Philadelphia. From there, he could keep an eye on the British.

More *Crisis* Papers

While the colonial army suffered at Valley Forge, General Howe's British army spent a comfortable winter in Philadelphia. There, they were fed and entertained by wealthy Loyalists in the city.

Confidence in Washington's leadership was at an all-time low. There were rumors of the army disbanding. Some officers urged that Washington be replaced by General Horatio Gates. Paine responded to the

Valley Forge
The American troops were in desperate straits the winter of 1777–1778. The men nearly froze from lack of clothes. They never had enough to eat, and most did not have shoes. The horses died of starvation, and the men were infected with a skin disease known as the itch. It was a low point for Washington's army.

rumors by writing *Crisis V*. It was printed in Lancaster, Pennsylvania, on March 21, 1778.

The first part of the pamphlet hurled insults at William Howe, commander of the British troops. He told Howe,

> Go home, sir, and endeavour to save the remains of your ruined country. . . . You are fighting for what you can never obtain, and we are defending what we never mean to part with. . . . Let England mind her own business and we will mind ours. Govern yourselves, and we will govern ourselves.[5]

Paine reminded American readers it was their duty to defend their country, and he urged them to stick together. He did not mention the misery of the troops at Valley Forge or the talk of replacing General George Washington.

At the end of January, Paine left Bordentown. He walked the one hundred twenty miles to York to resume his duties as secretary of the committee on foreign affairs.

Thomas Paine tried to encourage the American troops to persevere, even through their terrible winter encampment at Valley Forge.

Later in 1778, General Howe was replaced by General Henry Clinton, who moved the British troops from Philadelphia to New York. King George III sent a commission to America, promising to be easy on the colonists if they would give up the idea of independence. Paine published *Crisis VI* on October 28, 1788. The pamphlet attacked the commission and said that only independence would solve the problems between Great Britain and America.

Crisis VII, addressed to "The People of England," came out on November 21, 1778. It urged the British people to let the colonies go. Paine said that, when

Thomas Paine

children grow up and are ready to leave home, their parents bless them as they go. He believed nations should do the same with their colonies.

The Silas Deane Affair

At the same time, Silas Deane was in France, trying to obtain military supplies. Deane was a lawyer who had served twice as a delegate from Connecticut to the Continental Congress. He did not realize that the French government had already decided to help the colonies gain their independence from France's old enemy, England. However, the French wanted their aid to be kept a secret so as not to provoke war with England.

Deane met with Pierre-Augustin Caron de Beaumarchais, head of an organization set up by the French to secretly send supplies to the Americans. Within a few weeks, French ships loaded with guns, ammunition, and other supplies headed for America. Meanwhile, Paine heard from Arthur Lee, a Virginian who was with Benjamin Franklin in France. Lee said that the French government did not expect the Americans to pay for the supplies. France was sending them as a gift.

Deane and Beaumarchais were making a lot of money by charging high prices for the goods that were supposed to be a gift to America from France. At the end of 1777, the Continental Congress received a bill for 4.5 million livres (over $1 million), to be paid to France immediately. Deane sent a letter with it, saying the bill was correct.

Convinced that the facts were being covered up, Paine published an open letter to Deane in the

Pennsylvania Packet in December and followed it with several more. Paine believed Deane was unfit for public service. When Deane returned from France, he neglected to bring any of his papers with him. Paine wrote, "There is something in this concealment of papers that looks like an embezzlement."[6] Paine was later proven right, but not before he had suffered a great deal for criticizing Deane.

Paine was amazed at the hostility shown him by members of Congress and others for his attack on a fellow American patriot. He invited anyone who did not believe him to come to his office and see a report that said the supplies Deane claimed to have bought "were promised . . . as a present . . . before he ever arrived in France."[7]

France was embarrassed that the gift had been revealed. Conrad Alexandre Gérard, the French representative in America, demanded that Paine take back his accusations. Paine refused. In January 1779, John Penn of North Carolina moved in Congress that Paine be

Silas Deane, seen here, was angered by Thomas Paine's attempts to expose his corrupt dealings in France.

removed as the secretary of the committee for foreign affairs. The motion was seconded by Gouverneur Morris, but was bitterly debated for several hours.

The motion lost, but on January 8, Paine hand delivered a letter of resignation to Congress. In it, he denied any wrongdoing. Congress accepted his resignation and paid him the rest of his salary, two hundred fifty dollars, about ten weeks later.

Paine found employment as a clerk, and at the end of the year, he was appointed clerk of the Pennsylvania general assembly. In 1780, he helped write a bill that was introduced to ban slavery in Pennsylvania. It passed on March 1, 1780. During 1780, Paine also raised desperately needed money for George Washington's army. He convinced Philadelphia's wealthy merchants and traders to establish an army support fund, and he contributed the first $500 from his own meager savings. Paine also wrote three *Crisis* papers in 1780 (*Crisis VIII*, *Crisis IX*, and a special paper called *Crisis Extraordinary*). All three were written to improve the morale of the soldiers.

Paine also wrote an article that year called *Public Good*. It claimed that lands to the west of the colonies belonged to America as a whole, rather than to individual colonies. Virginia, which claimed most of this land, was very unhappy with Paine's proposal.

Paine was beginning to write articles that did not reflect public opinion as *Common Sense* had. The hero of the early years of the revolution was becoming a controversial figure.

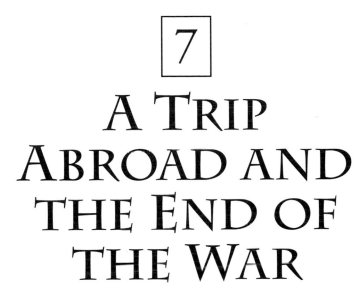

7

A Trip Abroad and the End of the War

In the fall of 1780, General Washington issued another desperate appeal for money and supplies for the Continental Army. On November 22, Congress decided to ask Louis XVI, king of France, for a loan of 25 million livres (French currency) in cash, or about $8 million. John Laurens would be sent as a special envoy to Paris.

Twenty-six-year-old Laurens was the son of Paine's close friend Henry Laurens, who had served as president of the Continental Congress. John Laurens had been an aide-de-camp to Washington. He and Paine had met three years before.

John Laurens spoke French well, but had no experience with diplomacy. He asked Paine to go along on the trip as his secretary.[1] Paine agreed.

However, Paine's enemies from the Silas Deane affair did not approve. Paine withdrew his request to serve as official secretary and said that he would pay his own way.[2] Before leaving, he wrote to General Nathanael Greene: "I leave America with the perfect satisfaction of having been to her an honest, faithful, and affectionate friend. I go away with the hope of returning to spend better or more agreeable days with her than those which are past."[3]

Mission to France

The men sailed to Europe on the *Alliance* in February 1781. Upon landing, the diplomats were greeted enthusiastically. Paine remarked that the French commandant "paid me great compliments on what he called the great success and spirit of my publications."[4] Wherever he went, Paine's fame preceded him. He was treated as a celebrity.

In Nantes, Paine was greeted at a reception as a hero. After more than a month on board ship, he was dressed in smelly clothes, suffered from the itch, and had long hair. However, he stood

Henry Laurens became one of Thomas Paine's strongest supporters.

proudly among the prominent citizens of the city. Elkanah Watson, who served as his interpreter, was embarrassed.

"I took the liberty," Watson recalled, "on his asking for the loan of a clean shirt, of speaking to him frankly of his dirty appearance and brimstone odor; and prevailed upon him to stew for an hour, in a hot bath."[5] At first, Paine refused, possibly thinking the bath would make his itch worse. Watson finally offered him a stack of recent English newspapers to look at in the bath, and Paine gave in.

Return to America

Paine so enjoyed the company and adulation of the French people that, after he and Laurens had succeeded in obtaining the loan, he considered staying in France. Laurens objected. He insisted that he needed Paine along in case of any personal misfortune.

Paine finally agreed, and they sailed on the French frigate *la Resolute* on June 1, bound for Philadelphia. The ship was accompanied by several gunboats and two brigs (two-masted ships with square rigged sails) loaded with clothing and military supplies. The frigate carried two huge double casks completely filled with silver. They made very slow progress, sailing in a zigzag route to avoid British ships.

Paine and Laurens learned from a passing vessel that the French Navy had not cleared Delaware Bay of British warships as they had hoped, so *la Resolute* changed course. The ship arrived in Boston on August 26.

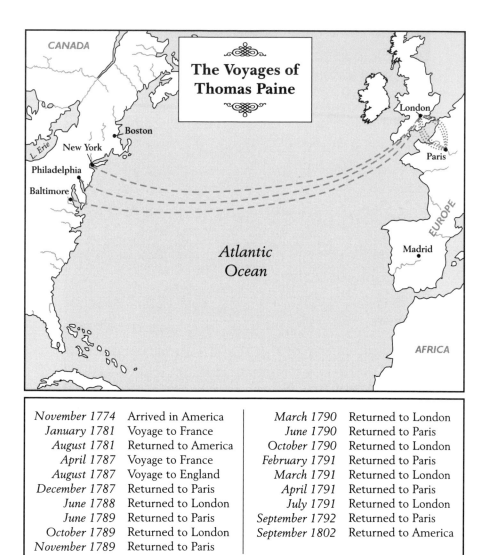

The Voyages of Thomas Paine

CANADA

L. Erie

Boston

New York

Philadelphia

Baltimore

London

Paris

EUROPE

Madrid

AFRICA

Atlantic Ocean

November 1774	Arrived in America		*March 1790*	Returned to London
January 1781	Voyage to France		*June 1790*	Returned to Paris
August 1781	Returned to America		*October 1790*	Returned to London
April 1787	Voyage to France		*February 1791*	Returned to Paris
August 1787	Voyage to England		*March 1791*	Returned to London
December 1787	Returned to Paris		*April 1791*	Returned to Paris
June 1788	Returned to London		*July 1791*	Returned to London
June 1789	Returned to Paris		*September 1792*	Returned to Paris
October 1789	Returned to London		*September 1802*	Returned to America
November 1789	Returned to Paris			

Thomas Paine made several voyages between Europe and America during the course of his career.

Sixteen teams of oxen moved the silver from Boston to Philadelphia. Most of the silver was used to fund the new Bank of North America. It was headed by Robert Morris, the superintendent of finance for the colonies.

Now that he and Paine had completed their mission, Laurens borrowed a horse and headed for Yorktown, Virginia, to help General Washington prepare for an encounter with British General Charles Cornwallis. Paine wanted to join them, but because he had no money, he returned to Philadelphia.

The Articles of Confederation, a plan of government for the new nation, had just been ratified. People increasingly believed that the Americans would win the war.

The Last Battle

Washington and Count de Grasse, the commander of the French fleet sent to help him, hoped to catch Cornwallis and his troops between the land and sea at Yorktown. The French fleet would be in the harbor. Washington's forces would march on land. Despite great odds, the plan worked. Washington's troops, with the help of the French, delivered a crushing defeat to the British. Cornwallis lost a large percentage of his seven thousand men. He was forced to surrender. It was the beginning of the end of the war.

Washington's army rode into Philadelphia in November. This time, it spent the winter enjoying the comforts of the city, while the British troops camped on Manhattan Island. Although the war was not officially

over, Philadelphia celebrated Washington's victory at Yorktown by decorating houses with ribbons and flags, setting off fireworks, and attending victory balls at night.

A New Job for Paine

Thomas Paine watched the victory parade from his room on Second Street. He was happy for the young country that he had helped create, but he himself was broke, depressed, and without a job. On November 3,

The American Revolution unofficially came to an end after the surrender of British General Charles Cornwallis's troops to American General George Washington.

he wrote to General Washington, bitterly describing his situation. He said that American officials were "cold and inattentive" and asked his old friend to try to pressure Congress into relieving his distress.[6]

Soon Robert Morris, Secretary for Foreign Affairs Robert Livingston, and General Washington offered Paine a job. He would write on behalf of independence, try to keep up morale, comment on military matters, and show the states that they needed to provide money for Congress and give it more power. For this, Paine would be paid $800 a year until the war formally ended. Paine agreed to the new job in February 1782. He met almost weekly with Morris, Livingston, and Washington, informing them of his ideas and getting their suggestions.

Crisis X, published in March 1782, urged the states to give Congress the power to levy taxes to pay for the war. *Crisis XI*, printed in May 1782, blasted England for its attempts to break up the alliance between France and America. *Crisis XII* was a reply to William Petty Fitzmorris, the Earl of Shelburne, who insisted that American independence would be financial ruin for Great Britain. Paine asked how America had become so important: "Was America, then, the giant of the empire, and England only her dwarf in waiting! Is the case so strangely altered, that those who once thought we could not live without them, are now brought to declare that they cannot exist without us?"[7]

This pamphlet received a mixed reception. Paine's old friend Nathanael Greene exclaimed, "Your fame

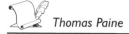

for your writings will be immortal!"[8] But Benjamin Franklin and Henry Laurens, who were trying to negotiate a peace deal with Great Britain, were irritated by it. Franklin remarked, "I should think now that we are studying peace and conciliation that you had as good not send to England the printed paper addressed to Lord Shelburne."[9]

More Problems in the Colonies

While Paine wrote about the problems of ending the war, other problems cropped up on the home front. Congress had requested the power to put a 5 percent tax on goods imported to America. The Rhode Island general assembly, comparing the measure with British tyranny, rejected it on November 1, 1782. In order for the tax to go into effect, all the states had to approve it.

Fulfilling the duties of his job, Paine wrote a series of letters to convince Rhode Island to accept the tax. These letters emphasized the fairness of the tax and the need for it. They were published in the *Providence Gazette* in December 1782 and January 1783.

Early in December, Paine hired a horse and set off for Providence. He did not know at the time that Virginia had withdrawn its approval of the tax issue.

Paine was met by hostility in Rhode Island. People accused him of being a "mercenary writer" (one who writes only for money), trying to help Congress make money. Some charged that he was trying to destroy Rhode Island. Tensions rose until Paine feared for his safety. After writing three more letters, he returned to Philadelphia.

It was March 1783. By this time, Maryland, North Carolina, and South Carolina had joined Virginia in repealing their acceptance of the tax.

The War Ends at Last

On April 11, 1783, the end of the war was officially announced. The Treaty of Paris had been signed by the United States, France, and Great Britain. Paine celebrated by writing the thirteenth and final *Crisis* paper. He ended it:

> But as the scenes of war are closed, and every man preparing for home and happier times, I therefore take my leave of the subject. I have most sincerely followed it from beginning to end, and through all its turns and windings: and whatever country I may hereafter be in, I shall always feel an honest pride at the part I have taken and acted, and a gratitude to nature and providence for putting it in my power to be of some use to mankind.[10]

Now that the war was over, Paine's agreement with Morris, Livingston, and Washington came to an end. He was left without a job. With no income, he was forced to move in with the Kirkbrides, his old friends in Bordentown, New Jersey. Paine launched a campaign for financial support from Congress, but it was blocked by enemies he had made during the Silas Deane affair.

In November 1783, after spending a month recuperating from scarlet fever, Paine was invited to

George Washington's Rocky Hill headquarters. He eagerly accepted the invitation. There, Paine enjoyed three weeks of good company, relaxation, and being pampered by servants. The men chatted about politics and science and performed a scientific experiment.

While Paine was at Rocky Hill, Washington received word that British troops were evacuating New York City. The two men rode to New York City on horseback. Together, they rode at the head of a celebratory parade. Paine was included in a grand public dinner that night, complete with booming cannons and toasts.

A few days later, when Washington left for his home at Mount Vernon, Virginia, Paine felt homeless and lost. Shortly after Christmas, he left New York City for Bordentown. He used money received from the French for writing in support of Franco-American relations to buy a small house near the Kirkbrides and a horse named Button.

Paine and Washington's Experiment
The local people insisted that the creek could be set on fire. Paine guessed that this was because there was natural gas beneath the creek bed. He and Washington sat at opposite ends of a boat, each holding a flaming roll of paper. Nothing happened until soldiers on shore stirred up the mud at the bottom of the creek with long sticks. Then fire leaped from Washington's torch to the surface of the water, proving that Paine was right.[11]

Americans everywhere rejoiced when they learned the news that the war had ended with an American victory.

A New Coat for Paine
One Sunday during Paine's visit at Rocky Hill, the weather was unusually mild. On the way to church, Paine left his heavy coat at the home of a nearby friend. When he returned in two hours, the man's servant had run off with the coat. Washington told him the moral of the story was, "It is necessary to watch as well as pray."[12] He gave Paine one of his own coats, and Paine wore it proudly for years.

Money and Property for Paine

Meanwhile, Washington urged Congress to vote Paine a gift of money for his contributions during the war. Paine also wrote to his friend, James Duane, the mayor of New York City, informing him of his need for money. Duane and Lewis Morris persuaded the New York legislature to award Paine some property in New Rochelle, New York.

In April 1784, Paine rode off on Button to inspect the three-hundred-acre farm. New Rochelle was a seaside township thirty miles northeast of New York City. The farm had been confiscated from a Loyalist, Frederick DaVoe, who had been caught escorting British troops through the area. He and his family had fled to Canada.

Paine officially received the property in a quiet ceremony on June 14, 1784. Paine was pleased and grateful, but he did not want to live in such a rural area. He also needed a cash income. Not wanting to sell the farm and appear ungrateful, he rented it and returned to Bordentown.

On April 9, 1785, the Pennsylvania general assembly awarded Paine five hundred pounds for his efforts during the war. They kept the amount relatively low, because legislation was still pending in Congress to pay him something.

In Virginia, Jefferson spoke in Paine's behalf in the Virginia general assembly. Washington also used his influence with friends there, writing,

> Can nothing be done for poor Paine? Must the merits, and Services of *Common Sense* continue to glide down the stream of time, unrewarded by this country? . . . His writings certainly have had a powerful effect upon the public mind; ought they not then to meet an adequate return? He is poor! He is chagreened [disappointed and embarrassed]! and almost, if not altogether, in despair of relief.[13]

James Madison, a member of the legislature, introduced legislation to give Paine land in Virginia worth at least four thousand pounds, but it was defeated. The legislature had not forgiven Paine for his attack on Virginia in *Public Good*.

In September, Paine wrote Congress, saying that it owed him at least six thousand dollars in expenses for his work during the Revolutionary War. He wrote, "I must declare to the Committee that it hurts me exceedingly to find, that after a service of so many years, and through such a perilous scene, I am now treated . . . as if I had no feelings to suffer or honour to preserve."[14]

On October 3, Congress voted to award Paine three thousand dollars for his contribution to the war effort. With these combined gifts, Paine could pay his bills and live comfortably.

Problems With the Bank of North America

About this time, controversy erupted over the Bank of North America. It had been founded four years earlier with part of the money Paine and Laurens brought back from France. The first deposit in the bank was five hundred dollars Paine had given to establish a subscription fund for the army (a fund to help buy supplies).

People were upset because coins were scarce and the bank refused to print paper money with which debts could be paid. Paine agreed with the bank. He believed paper money was worthless unless it was backed by gold or silver. The Pennsylvania general assembly voted to repeal the charter of the Bank of North America because it refused to accept $150,000 in worthless paper money authorized by the general assembly.

Paine wrote *Dissertation on Government; the Affairs of the Bank; and Paper Money* in February 1787. It said that the Pennsylvania general assembly's repeal of the charter was not legal. Eventually, the dispute was settled in the bank's favor when newly elected members of the assembly voted to write a new charter for the bank.

8

BRIDGING THE GAP BETWEEN AMERICA AND EUROPE

Now that the war was over and he had enough money to live on, Thomas Paine turned his thoughts toward science. He and Joseph Kirkbride shared a love of science and inventing. They set up a lab on Kirkbride's property in Bordentown, New Jersey, where they could do experiments.

Paine spent most of his time designing a single-span iron bridge. He was not good with his hands, however, so he hired John Hall, a recent immigrant from England, to help him build models of the bridges he designed.

Paine's Iron Bridge

Paine got the idea for his bridge as he observed huge chunks of ice floating down the Schuylkill River.

Bridges of the time were set on piers driven into the river bottom. They could be easily damaged by ice. Most bridges were built with wood. They were cheap to build but rotted easily and did not last.

Paine's inspiration for a new kind of bridge was a spider web. He said, "I naturally supposed that when nature enabled that insect to make a web she taught it the best method of putting it together."[1] Paine's bridge had an arch made of a number of separate sections, with interlocking ribs. It could be assembled and disassembled, so it could be moved.

Together, Paine and Hall made three small-scale models of the bridge, one wooden, one cast iron, and one wrought iron. The Pennsylvania general assembly planned to erect a bridge across the Schuylkill River, and Paine hoped it would use his design. He reported that it would cost about $33,330 to build in the money of the time.

Paine loaded the completed models onto a cart and took them to Philadelphia. There, they were displayed in Benjamin Franklin's backyard. In December 1786, Paine demonstrated the strength of the wrought iron model by having three men stand on it. On New Year's Day, the model was put on exhibit at the Pennsylvania state house. However, it failed to attract any investors.

Franklin suggested that Paine get the bridge approved by the French Academy of Sciences and the British Royal Academy.[2] Franklin gave him letters of introduction to several prominent French politicians and scientists. Paine also wanted to visit his parents. He had been away for thirteen years.

Off to France and England

He sailed for France on April 26. He was fifty years old. When he arrived in Paris in the early summer of 1787, the political scene was unstable. King Louis XVI was weak and his queen, Marie Antoinette, was unpopular. Unemployment was widespread. The Roman Catholic Church and the wealthy were corrupt. The restless middle class wanted power. The country was close to bankruptcy, and France and England were again on the brink of war.

While in France, Paine wrote a pamphlet called *Prospects on the Rubicon*. In it, he argued that the cost of war always fell on the poor. "I defend the cause of the poor, of the manufacturers, of the tradesmen, of the farmers, and of all those on whom the real burden of taxes falls—but above all, I defend the cause of humanity," he wrote.[3]

The Marquis de Lafayette was one of the most important leaders in France at the time. He and Paine had met in Philadelphia. Lafayette was also a hero to the

The weak monarchy of King Louis XVI caused widespread problems throughout France that would eventually erupt in revolution.

American people. At the age of twenty, he had fought alongside George Washington in the American Revolution. He had been wounded at Brandywine.

Now Paine was accepted into Lafayette's circle of friends. He enjoyed life in Paris to the fullest. He discussed politics with Lafayette, dined with the aristocracy, and talked science with prominent scientists.[4]

Paine presented his model bridge to the French Academy of Sciences on July 21. On August 29, they gave a favorable report, saying that, of all the models and plans for iron bridges they had seen, Paine's was the simplest, strongest, and lightest.

Paine was delighted with the endorsement. He went to England on August 30, 1787. When he traveled to Thetford, he learned that his father had died several months earlier, at the age of seventy-nine. He spent three weeks with his ninety-year-old mother. Before he left, he arranged for her to

The Marquis de Lafayette became a political leader in France after serving brilliantly as an aide to General Washington during the American Revolution.

receive a pension of nine shillings a week for the rest of her life.

Politics in England

Henry Laurens had written a letter of introduction for Paine to Edmund Burke, a prominent member of the British Parliament. Burke was from Ireland, and his manners were not as polished as many other members of Parliament. However, his brilliant mind and eloquent speeches won him respect. He had spoken out against the Stamp Act, and said that Great Britain should give the American colonies their independence.

Burke invited Paine to spend a week at his home and introduced him to many prominent Whigs, the party then in power. The Whigs wanted to restore trade with America. They thought Paine might be influential in helping them. The Whigs entertained him lavishly and praised his writing.

The Whigs overlooked Paine's rough manners and appearance in the hopes he could help them. Paine, however, had his own ideas. He favored a revolution in England and believed that the English should call a national convention and write a new constitution. King George III had spells of madness and Paine believed he was not fit to run the country.[5]

William Pitt was the British prime minister (chief executive), and Paine and Burke were united in their hatred of him. Burke, however, was not as radical as Paine. He did not believe in revolutions. He preferred gradual change through legislation.

Paine's Appearance

Paine, in his coarse homespun clothing and his unpowdered crooked wig, made a startling contrast to the gentlemen entertaining him. His pants always needed pressing and his black socks drooped. At this time in English life, elegant grooming among the upper class was considered important.[6]

Paine considered himself a sort of unofficial ambassador to England.[7] He kept Thomas Jefferson, the American representative in Paris, informed about events in London. Paine hoped to be appointed ambassador to France, but the position was given to Gouverneur Morris, Paine's old adversary. Morris disapproved of Paine's radical ideas and considered him low class.

Building the Bridge

Paine presented his bridge model to the Royal Society in London. The society approved the plan, and he secured British patents on the design on August 26, 1788. (A patent protects the right of an inventor to make, sell, and use his or her product exclusively.)

Paine and Burke toured iron factories in England, searching for someone to build the bridge. The Walker brothers of Sheffield agreed to construct an experimental span at their works in Rotherham. Paine would supervise the building of the ninety-foot arch.

The bridge was shipped in pieces to London in the spring of 1789. It was exhibited near Paddington, now part of London. Many thought it was a fine design, but no one was willing to finance the venture.

Trouble in France

While Paine dabbled in English politics, great changes were taking place in France. On July 14, 1789, angry mobs stormed the Bastille, the notorious Paris prison, and freed the prisoners. This was significant, not because of the seven prisoners who were freed, but because it showed that the common people could not be controlled by the government.

A bad harvest had caused a famine in the country, and the poor were driven to violence, looting homes and burning places where documents were stored. The poor and the middle class had been kept down too long. They had finally rebelled.

On October 5, a mob marched on the palace at Versailles and forced the king and queen to return with the people to Paris. Paine decided to go back to Paris and take part in the revolution. At the time, the only American in Paris with diplomatic status was Gouverneur Morris. He was there on an official mission in connection with payment of the American debt to France. Although they were not friends, Paine stayed with Morris.

Lafayette was pleased to have Paine back in Paris. He presented Paine with the key to the Bastille to send to George Washington, as a symbolic gift from one free nation to another.

On July 14, 1789, the French Revolution began when peasants stormed the Bastille.

By March 1790, Paine was back in London, seeing to his bridge. When he arrived, he sent the Bastille key to Washington, along with a note that spoke of his happiness with the apparent success of the revolution. Paine believed the French Revolution would soon create a republic like that of the United States. He was wrong.

9

ENGLAND AND FRANCE TURN AGAINST PAINE

⸺⚬⚬⚬⸺

Thomas Paine was angry when he read Edmund Burke's book, *Reflections on the Revolution in France*, in November 1790. The book took a hostile view of the French Revolution. It was written to alert the English aristocracy about what could happen if the poor took over.

Burke's main point was the certain failure of any attempt to extend the effects of the American and French revolutions to England. He said that the people of England "look upon the legal hereditary succession of their crown as among their rights, not as among their wrongs; as a benefit, not as a grievance."[1] The book received tremendous praise.

Rights of Man

Paine immediately set to work writing *Rights of Man*. In it, he refuted Burke's argument. He wrote, "As it is my design to make those that can scarcely read understand, I shall therefore avoid every literary ornament and put it in language as plain as the alphabet."[2] The direct contrast between Paine's down-to-earth style and the flowery prose Burke used was deliberate. Paine's new book was designed to appeal to self-educated artisans and working people, who, in turn, could pass on its ideas to those who could not read.

Paine worked feverishly. In less than three months, Part I of *Rights of Man* was finished. It said that America was the only country in the world where kings did not repress and take advantage of the people.

Monarchy, Paine stated, makes individuals afraid to think and suspicious of others. Under these circumstances, the natural rights of the individual—freedom of speech, assembly, and religion—are repressed.

Paine also condemned war. He thought a democratic government would be less prone to war. He said that the only effective government was self-government.

He believed that all people, whether male or female, black or white, rich or poor, young or old, were born with equal natural rights. Everyone should be able to act freely as long as they did not injure or trespass on the natural rights of others. He dedicated the book to George Washington.

Paine finished the manuscript on January 29, 1791, his fifty-fourth birthday. London printer Joseph Johnson promised to have it ready in time for Washington's birthday and the opening of the British Parliament on February 22.

However, government agents who had heard about the manuscript were harassing Johnson. On the day it was supposed to come out, Johnson decided not to release it. Paine quickly found another printer, J. S. Jordan. The book was finally published on March 13. It caused a great commotion in England, as Paine had hoped it would.

Rights of Man sparked a fiery debate about political principles. It also made Paine the most controversial figure in England. People attacked his writing as vulgar, a word that comes from the word *vulgus*, meaning common people. That was exactly who Paine was trying to reach.

Writer Isaac Hunt condemned Paine for his "coarse and rustic style." He was afraid the "illiterate and unskilled" readers "may easily be duped to think seditiously [against the government], and of course to act rebelliously according to his wishes."[3]

No book had ever sold like *Rights of Man*. The first printing sold out in three days. By the time the sixth printing came out in May, fifty thousand copies had already been sold. The younger William Pitt, now prime minister, was alarmed, but was afraid that arresting Paine would make him a hero. Pitt told a friend, "Paine is quite right, but what am I to do? As

things are, if I were to encourage Tom Paine's opinions I should have a bloody revolution."[4]

Back to France

In mid-April, Paine went to France to arrange for *Rights of Man* to be translated into French and published there. He renewed his acquaintance with French and Americans there, including Gouverneur Morris.

Paine was convinced that the French Revolution would be a repeat of the American Revolution. He did not see that the splits between people would to lead to violence. There was such a big gap between the poor and the wealthy aristocracy, that it was just a matter of time before the poor rose up and tried to take control. Thomas Paine soon experienced violence firsthand.

He was still in bed on June 21, 1791, when the Marquis de Lafayette burst into his room, shouting, "The birds are flown! The birds are flown!" Lafayette was referring to the fact that King Louis XVI and his family had fled Paris to get away from the people, who wanted to keep the royal family under close guard. Paine quickly dressed and the two men joined the crowd gathering in the street.[5]

Everyone wore the revolutionary cockades (knots of ribbon) in their hats, a sign that they supported the revolution. Paine had run into the street without his hat, so the crowd thought he was a Royalist. Thinking he was sympathetic to the king, they began attacking him. He protested that he was an American as they punched and kicked him and tore his clothes. He did not speak French, and if someone in the crowd had not translated his remarks, he might have been hanged from the nearest lamppost.[6]

The people showed their anger at the king's escape by smashing windows and inn signs that bore the king's name or the fleur-de-lis, the symbol of the royal family. The king's secret papers, in which he condemned the revolution, were discovered, and people demanded that he step down from the throne.

Paine and four friends founded the Société des republicains (Society of Republicans) "to enlighten minds about republicanism."[7] The society issued a proclamation calling for a republic and saying King Louis no longer had any authority. Early on the morning of July 1, the society posted the proclamation on walls all over Paris and nailed copies of it to the doors of the hall where the National Assembly, the French lawmaking body, would meet that day.

Part II of *Rights of Man*

On July 8, Paine returned to England. The political scene there was not much better. He had been invited to speak at a dinner in Birmingham for supporters of the French Revolution on July 14, the anniversary of the storming of the Bastille. It was canceled because the government put pressure on the landlord of the inn where it was to be held.

Rights of Man had influenced many, and Prime Minister Pitt was worried. For a time, he decided not to attack Paine openly. Instead, he started a campaign

behind the scenes to ruin Paine's reputation with the people of England.

Pitt paid George Chalmers to write a hostile biography of Paine. Writing under the name of Francis Oldys, Chalmers dug up unknown details of Paine's life (including lies about his marriage), criticized his poor English, and gave him little credit for contributing anything to society.

During the autumn of 1791, Paine worked on Part II of *Rights of Man*. Meanwhile, Edmund Burke published a reply to the first part of *Rights of Man*. In it, he implied that the arguments Paine had put forth were not even worth refuting.

Printers Johnson and Jordan both refused to print Part II. They feared they would be imprisoned. Finally, Thomas Chapman, a Paine admirer, agreed to print it.

When Chapman had about one hundred pages printed, he read some of the proofs, and decided the book was too dangerous to publish. Paine was upset, but finally made a deal with Jordan and Johnson. He agreed to take full legal responsibility for the contents of the book. *Rights of Man, Part the Second* came out on February 16, 1792, with a dedication to the Marquis de Lafayette.

The British government was becoming more worried about Paine's influence on the English people. On May 21, 1792, King George III issued a proclamation against writings that criticized the government. Bookshop owners were harassed by agents of the police. Some were imprisoned or fined for selling Paine's book.

Sales of *Rights of Man*

One hundred thousand copies of the two-part edition were sold in the United States. Part II sold two hundred thousand copies in England, Scotland, and Wales in its first year of publication. It also sold well in Ireland.

But it was extremely controversial. Soon after Part II appeared, Gouverneur Morris arrived in London on his way to Paris, where he would be minister to France. He wrote to George Washington: "I have read Paine's new publication today, and tell him I am really afraid that he will be punished."[8]

That same day, Paine received a summons to appear in court on charges of seditious libel—false writings against the government. He was accused of "being a wicked, malicious, seditious, and ill-disposed person."[9]

Spies constantly followed Paine. Posters condemning him were hung on London walls. Hostility was growing. In several towns, dummies representing Paine were hanged or burned in effigy. Pitt soon arrested Jordan for printing Part II. Police raided bookshops all over the country and seized copies of the book.

To Paine, this was proof that he was succeeding in enlightening the people. Friends worried about him, but he laughed them off. He believed the libel trial would be a chance to present his ideas to the world.

He called openly on the British people to support the French Revolution.

Escape to France

In early September 1792, Paine learned that he had been offered French citizenship and elected to the French National Convention, the lawmaking body for the new French republic. On September 13, while at dinner with friends, William Blake, Paine's friend and fellow writer, warned him that orders had been given in England to arrest him and seize his papers. "You must not go home, or you are a dead man," Blake said.[10]

Late that evening, Paine left with two friends for the English Channel, where he could get a boat to France. A few minutes after they sailed, two couriers on horseback galloped up to the pier with a warrant for Paine's arrest.

When Paine arrived in Calais, France, on September 13, he was given a hero's welcome. People gathered at the town hall that evening to honor him. Several days later, he went to Paris and found the city in a state of chaos.

Two weeks earlier, the convention had declared the country a republic and ousted the king. In June, eight thousand people armed with pikes (spears), muskets, and pitchforks invaded the assembly. Paine thought these problems were just a temporary product of change.

On September 19, Paine took his seat in the convention. The legislators were debating what to do about the king. The Jacobins, who were radicals, wanted to kill him. The Girondins, who believed in slow, orderly change, favored letting him live. Paine agreed with the Girondins. On November 6, a commission presented its report on the king, saying he deserved to die. On January 18, the majority of the legislature voted for the death penalty.

Paine wrote a speech, which was translated into French and read by someone standing with him before the assembly. He said that the king was no longer a threat to anyone. He hoped the assembly would reconsider its verdict.

The speech had little influence. On January 21, 1793, Thomas Paine, along with thousands of Parisians, watched as King Louis XVI was led to the guillotine to be beheaded. Paine was beginning to doubt the success of the revolution.

The Girondin party began to disintegrate in the spring of 1793, under pressure from the radical Jacobins. Early in October, most of the Girondin leaders were imprisoned, and on October 31, they were executed. After this, Paine was the only anti-Jacobin not in jail. But his freedom would not last long.

Paine Is Imprisoned

On September 29, a committee was elected to rewrite the French Constitution. Condorcet, a Girondin member of the assembly, and Paine did most of the writing.

Paine was also writing *The Age of Reason*, which set forth his philosophy of religion. In it, he attacked all organized religions. He had often been shocked at the way clergymen said that the plight of the poor was the

will of God. He disagreed with Edmund Burke that church and state should be united.

On Christmas Eve, Paine heard the results of his trial in England, which had been held in his absence on December 19. As he expected, he was convicted. The jury had been handpicked by the government. It consisted of wealthy men who were hostile to Paine. To everyone's surprise, several thousand of Paine's supporters had gathered outside the Guildhall where the trial was held. They chanted, "Paine for ever!" and "Paine and the Liberty of the press."[11]

Although initially just a fight to win more rights for the common people, the French Revolution soon became violent. Political leaders, including the king and queen, were executed.

The manuscript of *The Age of Reason* was finished on December 27. That same day, the French Committee of General Security issued a warrant for Paine's arrest. In the middle of the night, the police appeared at his door. He asked for permission to turn over his manuscript to Joel Barlow, an American friend living in Paris. It was granted. Later that night, the doors of Luxembourg Prison slammed behind him. A ten-month nightmare began.

While Paine was in prison, Barlow was able to get *The Age of Reason* printed. Copies of the book soon appeared in America. This book created the greatest uproar of any of Paine's writings. Ministers were appalled. They accused him of being an atheist. His good reputation in the United States began to melt away.

Meanwhile, Paine suffered in the cold, damp, dimly lit stone building of Luxembourg Prison. For most, the Luxembourg was a mere stopping place on the way to the guillotine. The Reign of Terror, the phase of the French Revolution during which at least seventeen thousand people believed to be enemies of the republic were executed, was in full swing.

When news of Paine's imprisonment spread through Paris, the Americans living there took a petition to Gouverneur Morris, asking him to secure Paine's release. Morris stalled, saying that Paine had become a Frenchman. He told the French foreign minister that his government did not feel responsible for Paine.

Gouverneur Morris, an American statesman and Paine's old enemy, did little to help get Thomas Paine released from prison in France.

Because France wanted to maintain good relations with the United States, Morris could have put some pressure on the government to release him. But he did not. Morris wrote to Thomas Jefferson, who had just resigned as secretary of state, saying, "I incline to think that if he is quiet in prison he may have the good luck to be forgotten, whereas should he be brought into much notice, the long suspended axe may fall on him."[12] Jefferson agreed that Paine's best chance of survival was to lie low.

In prison, Paine wrote a long, detailed attack on the Bible, claiming that it was not the word of God.

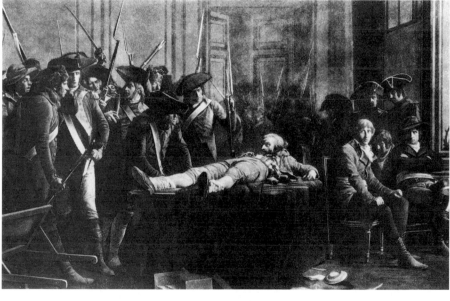

Thomas Paine was saved from execution when Robespierre, the leader of the French Revolution, was himself arrested (seen here, lying on the table) and executed.

Paine's Brush With Death

Paine later described the evening when he was almost taken to be executed:

> One hundred and sixty-eight persons were taken out of the Luxembourg in one night, and one hundred and sixty of them guillotined the next day, of which I knew I was to be one, and the manner I escaped that fate is curious, and has all the appearance of an accident. The room in which I lodged was on the ground floor, one of a long range under a gallery, and the door opened outward and flat against the wall. . . . When persons by scores and hundreds were taken out for the guillotine it was always done by night, and those who performed that office had a private mark or sign by which they knew what rooms to go to and what number to take. We were four, and the door of our room was marked, unobserved by us, with that number, in chalk; but it happened, if happening is the proper word, that the door was open and flat against the wall, and thereby the mark came inside when we shut it at night; and the destroying angel passed us by.[13]

He did not believe Christ was the son of God, but still considered him a great man. He made it clear that he was not an atheist, however, saying, "I believe in one God, and no more; and I hope for happiness beyond this life."[14]

Paine lost several cellmates to the guillotine, and in June 1794, it seemed he would meet the same fate. Maximilien Robespierre, the head of the government at the time, had signed a warrant for Paine's execution. Paine was lucky—he escaped the death sentence when Robespierre himself was arrested.

Soon after this close call, Robespierre was guillotined. Thomas Paine was out of immediate danger. However, he had been in prison for six months and was eager to be free.

10

BETTER TIMES IN FRANCE

It was July 1794. Although his life was no longer in danger, Thomas Paine was still in prison in Paris. The damp conditions and lack of fresh air were taking their toll on his health, and he longed for freedom.

The French translation of *The Age of Reason* had just been published. Apparently, Paine's friends had waited until Robespierre was executed so they would not attract unwanted attention to Paine.[1]

Through it all, Paine continued writing. He revised *Rights of Man* and added a new preface. He also wrote poetry, reminiscences, an *Essay on Aristocracy*, and an *Essay on the Character of Robespierre*.

He also spent much of his time trying to gain his release from prison. He wrote to both the National

Convention and the Committee of Public Safety. They did not answer.

Monroe's Appointment Brings Hope

When Paine heard in August that his old antagonist Gouverneur Morris had been replaced as American minister to France by James Monroe, he thought his release was in sight. He immediately wrote to Monroe. Paine heard that he was no longer considered an American citizen, and he frantically penned a forty-three-page letter crammed with legal and philosophical arguments confirming his citizenship.

On October 4, he received Monroe's reply. Monroe assured Paine that he considered him a United States citizen. "By being with us through the revolution," he wrote, "you are of our country as absolutely as if you had been born there."[2]

Paine's reply included a model letter that Monroe could submit to the French Committee of General Security, which was in charge of releasing prisoners. Monroe wrote a more tactful letter of his own to the committee. On November 4, he received the order for Paine's release.

Monroe went to the Luxembourg to pick up Paine, then took him to his house to stay. He was shocked by the gray-bearded Paine's haggard and stooped appearance.[3] The invitation to stay with Monroe was probably intended as a temporary measure, but a year later, Paine was still living with the Monroes. Monroe wrote that Paine would continue to be his guest "till his

death or departure for America, however remote either the one or the other event may be."[4]

Paine's advice was useful to Monroe. He knew the people and politics of France well. However, he could not let go of his bitterness toward the United States for letting him languish in prison for ten months. Soon after he was released, he wrote a letter to President George Washington, protesting his neglect in this matter. Washington ignored it, but Monroe was embarrassed to have Paine attacking the United States while living with him and his family.

Back to the National Convention

In December 1794, Thomas Paine was restored to the National Convention, which was preparing to write a new constitution for the French Republic. He was also given eighteen hundred livres in back pay, which was owed to him for his time in prison.

Paine wrote a speech urging the convention to include universal suffrage, or the right for all men to vote, in the constitution. He was against the requirement that a man must own property in order to vote. He wrote that this "is dangerous and impolitic, sometimes ridiculous, and always unjust."[5] The convention remained unconvinced.

Soon after, Paine became seriously ill and had to stay in bed. He had an abscess on his side left from his prison days. It had never healed. He was deathly pale and helpless, and everyone believed he was about to die.

James Monroe, who later became president of the United States, was
a firm supporter of Paine. Thomas Paine lived with Monroe's family
when he was first released from prison.

Paine finally regained his health, but became more and more unhappy with the United States government in general, and George Washington in particular. The ratification of the Jay Treaty between the United States and England further angered him. The terms of the treaty were favorable to England. It gave the British the right to impound, or take over, American ships trading with countries Great Britain was at war with. England was also allowed to force American sailors to join the royal navy. These terms effectively cut off all trade between the United States and France.

Letter to George Washington

In the spring of 1796, Paine left Monroe's house not long before publication of his *Letter to George Washington*. This was a long open letter that Paine sent to Benjamin Franklin Bache, Benjamin Franklin's

Paine Blames Washington for His Illness

Paine wrote to United States Congressman James Madison, "I owe this illness (from which I have not much prospect of recovering) partly to Robespierre and partly to Mr. Washington. He ought to have said to somebody—inquire into the case of Mr. Paine and see if there is anything we can do for him."[6] Paine resented the fact that Washington, now president of the United States, had not made more of an effort to help Paine get released from prison.

grandson. Bache published an excerpt in October, another just before elections in November, and the entire pamphlet in February 1797.

The letter was seventy pages long. About half of it focused on the Jay Treaty. Addressing President Washington, Paine wrote,

> And as to you, sir, treacherous in private friendship (for so you have been to me, and that in the day of danger) and a hypocrite in public life, the world will be puzzled to decide whether you are an apostate [renegade] or an imposter; whether you have abandoned good principles or whether you ever had any.[7]

He went on to attack Washington's reputation as a military leader.

The letter aroused great controversy in the United States. Washington was still extremely popular, even though some people said he was too aristocratic and aloof and that he neglected the old soldiers from the revolution. The Jay Treaty was unpopular and had damaged the president's reputation.

However, even many of the people who did not like Washington thought Paine should not have launched such a violent attack on someone in a high office. Many were also disenchanted with Paine because of his attacks on religion in *The Age of Reason*.

Washington himself ignored the letter at first. Later, he described it as a lie inspired by the French. In defense of Washington, he may not have even known that Paine was imprisoned. He also may have believed Morris's contention that Paine would be safer if no attention were called to him.

Life With the Bonnevilles

Meanwhile, Paine moved in with the family of Nicolas de Bonneville in Paris. Bonneville was the printer who had published Part II of *Rights of Man* in French. Paine was a regular contributor to Bonneville's liberal republican newspaper, *Le Bien Informé* (*The Well Informed*).

Paine enjoyed life with the Bonnevilles immensely. He enjoyed the company of the Bonneville children, one of whom was named after him. He continued his routine of sleeping late, reading the paper, and chatting with visitors. He always took a nap after lunch, then went for a walk.

Paine's interest turned again to his bridge design. It had finally been used to build a bridge across the river Wear in Sunderland, England, but he received no money, because he was a fugitive from England. He worked to improve the design, making models in pasteboard, then in lead.

Joel Barlow, the poet from Connecticut, was probably Paine's closest friend during this period. Barlow was also interested in science. Robert Fulton, who would be the first person to operate steamboats commercially, also became a close friend. He and Paine spent hours arguing the merits of steam power. Fulton believed he could power a boat with steam, while Paine doubted it.

Paine also spent a lot of time in cafés, conversing with Irish revolutionaries, who wanted to overthrow British government in Ireland. Theobald Wolfe Tone was one of the leaders of the movement. He liked Paine, praised his conversation, and said his humor was witty.

In 1797, Paine decided to publish *Agrarian Justice*, which he had written during the winter of 1795–1796 while convalescing from his illness. It was a protest against the landed aristocracy who ruled France. He argued against poverty and stated that those with property had an obligation to help the poor. He called for an old-age pension for people over fifty. He also suggested a one-time payment of fifteen pounds to all young people upon reaching the age of twenty-one. This would help them get started when they left home.

In November 1797, James Monroe learned that he was being recalled to the United States. He would be replaced as ambassador by Charles Pinckney. The Monroes urged Paine to go back to the United States with them. He traveled as far as Le Havre, but seeing the British frigates in the English Channel just outside French territorial waters, he changed his mind. He felt that, as long as the British government could stop American ships, it was not safe to sail for home. He later heard that Monroe's ship had been stopped en route to the United States by a British warship "that searched every part of it, and down to the hold, for Thomas Paine."[8] He returned to Paris in early summer, postponing his return to America until a peace treaty could be signed with Great Britain.

Napoleon Takes Over as Emperor

In November 1799, Napoleon Bonaparte, a general in the French Army, seized power in France. Paine had met him several years earlier when the general came to the Bonnevilles' home. Napoleon was eager to get into

Paine's good graces. He thought Paine might be useful to him in the future. He told Paine that *Rights of Man* had influenced him greatly, and he slept every night with a copy under his pillow. He also told the writer that a statue of gold should be erected to him in every city in the universe.[9] Paine was flattered and liked Napoleon at once.

Paine had been working on plans for an invasion of England since 1796, hoping to start a revolution there. Napoleon was interested in the plan and invited Paine to take part in it when it came about. Paine, however, did not think it would succeed. He did not think the English people would rise up against the government and support the French. This angered Napoleon. He later abandoned the plan and never spoke to Paine again. Paine also became disenchanted with him.

Paine spent the winter of 1799 and 1800 in Belgium visiting Joseph Van Huele, his former cellmate at the Luxembourg. Van Huele introduced him to many prominent Belgians.

When he returned to Paris in April, Paine was told "that the police are informed that he is behaving irregularly and that at the first complaint against him he will be sent back to America."[10] Apparently, Napoleon's government had decided that Paine might be dangerous. The warning was effective. For the next eighteen months, Paine did practically no political writing.

Paine also learned that George Washington had died the previous December. Napoleon called for ten days of mourning, saying that Washington's "memory will forever be dear to the French people."[11] Paine spent the

Napoleon Bonaparte, the dictator who ended the French Revolution by taking power in France, is seen here in a painting by Antoine-Jean Gros.

next year afraid to stir up controversy, yet unable to return to America.

In October 1800, he learned that Thomas Jefferson would probably be elected president. He immediately wrote to him. In March, the new president replied to Paine's letters, inviting him to return to the United States on the American warship *Maryland*.

News of the letter leaked out to the press, and was publicized in the *National Intelligencer and Advertiser*. Jefferson's enemies jumped on the story and criticized him for wanting to bring "the loathesome Thomas Paine, a drunken atheist" back to the United States.[12] Not wanting to embarrass his friend further, Paine turned down the offer.

In March 1802, a peace treaty was signed between the French and the English, ending a European war brought on by the French Revolution. It was finally safe for Paine to return to America.

His old friend Clio Rickman came from England to see him off. The two enjoyed a few days together, reliving old times. Finally, on September 2, Paine boarded a ship for the United States. He took with him his personal belongings, the ship models, and cartons of personal papers. After an absence of fifteen years, Thomas Paine was finally returning to America.

11

LATER YEARS IN AMERICA

The United States had changed while Thomas Paine was in Europe. Its opinion of him had changed, too. He had left a hero and returned a controversial figure. His reputation had been tarnished by his *Letter to George Washington* and *The Age of Reason*.

Paine's supporters worried that the bitterness people felt toward him might make it unsafe for him to return. But when he landed in Baltimore, Maryland, on October 30, 1802, he was greeted enthusiastically. There were no unpleasant incidents.

Soon, however, critical stories appeared in newspapers in New York, Philadelphia, and Baltimore. President Jefferson was also viciously attacked for inviting Paine to return.

Paine remained silent at first. He tolerated the abuse because he believed strongly in freedom of the press. He wrote to Clio Rickman, "You can have no idea of the agitation which my arrival occasioned. From New Hampshire to Georgia . . . every newspaper was filled with applause or abuse."[1]

A few days later, Paine traveled to Washington, D.C., where Jefferson welcomed him. One newspaper described Paine:

> Years have made more impression on his body than his mind. He bends a little forward, carries one hand in the other behind, when he walks. . . . His conversation is uncommonly interesting; he is gay, humorous, and full of anecdote . . . his memory preserves its full capacity, and his mind is irresistible.[2]

Jefferson, ignoring the uproar, invited Paine to dine with him at the Executive Mansion, as the White House was then called. The two men were often seen walking through the streets together, engaged in conversation.

Paine's familiarity with France enabled him to advise Jefferson on French affairs. His input was especially helpful as the United States negotiated with the French to buy the Louisiana Territory, which would almost double the size of the nation.

Living in Bordentown

Paine was running short of money again, so he could no longer remain in Washington, D.C. Madame Marguerite Bonneville, the wife of Paine's French friend Nicolas, and her three boys had arrived in America in November.

Paine had paid their passage and set them up in his Bordentown house.

In February, he headed for Bordentown, stopping in Philadelphia to visit old friends. Some, including Benjamin Rush, were decidedly cool. They had been put off by *The Age of Reason*. Charles Willson Peale, an artist friend, however, was glad to see Paine and showed him his new museum, located in the hall of the American Philosophical Society. He asked Paine if he could display his bridge models. Paine agreed.

Back in Bordentown, Paine stayed with the Kirkbrides. A few days later, he was off for New York. He was honored at a banquet given by the Republicans, the political party headed by James Madison and Thomas Jefferson. Several rallies were also held in his behalf. He met with James Monroe, who had been appointed special emissary to France to help complete the Louisiana Purchase. Paine gave him a letter of introduction to a man in Paris who was knowledgeable about Louisiana.

Back in Bordentown, Paine continued writing his series of *Letters to the Citizens of the United States*, which he had begun in November. The letters appeared in the *National Intelligencer* in Washington. In them, Paine defended his beliefs about religion and politics.

Meanwhile, Paine still hoped to get his bridge erected over the Schuylkill River, and sent Congress an essay on the subject, *The Construction of Iron Bridges*. Congress turned down the request.

That same summer, the press falsely reported that he had tried in 1794 to organize a French invasion to "revolutionize" the United States. The rumors stopped only after he threatened court action if the story persisted.

At the end of August 1803, Paine traveled to Stonington, Connecticut, to visit his friend Captain Nathan Haley. A steady stream of fishermen, farmers, and artisans came to meet him. While he was there, he arranged for the education of his godson, Thomas Paine Bonneville.

Winter in New Rochelle

At the end of the New England autumn, Paine headed for his New Rochelle farm for the winter. He planned to build a new house. His old home had burned to the ground while he was in France. He would pay for the new house by cutting wood and selling it in New York. Meanwhile, he would live in a little cottage on the property.

Unfortunately, soon after his arrival he was struck by a severe attack of gout, an inflammation of the joints. He was unable to walk and could not use his hands. Seeing that he could not manage alone, Captain Daniel Pelton, who ran a general store in New Rochelle, invited Paine to stay with him. Paine went gladly and the gout soon improved. However, two weeks later, Paine fell and was badly shaken and bruised.

Mr. Staple, one of Pelton's clerks, offered to care for Paine. For two months, Paine did nothing but eat and sleep. He became depressed when he received news that his dear friend Joseph Kirkbride had died. He began drinking brandy to kill his pain.

On sunny days, Paine sat on the porch of the store and talked to people. The passersby enjoyed his conversation and remarked on his cheerfulness. Paine thrived on the attention.

Still unable to use his hands, he dictated an essay, *To the People of England on the Invasion of England*, to a scribe. It warned the English people of a possible attack by Napoleon and appeared in the *Philadelphia Aurora* on March 6, 1804. This seemed to be more an attempt to prove to the English that he had been right than an attempt to help them.

Feeling better, Paine moved to New York, where he got rooms in a boardinghouse for himself and the Bonnevilles. He became irritated with Madame Bonneville when she ran up bills in his name. He refused to pay and the landlord sued him. Paine won, but he decided to pay the bills anyway.

Paine's Condition Deteriorates

While in New York, he became friendly with Elihu Palmer, who published a journal called *The Prospect*. Paine wrote seventeen articles for the journal, defending deism (belief in an impersonal god) and attacking organized religion.

He had many friends in New York, but was often insulted in the streets. The press continued to attack him. He was called an alcoholic and an infidel, or religious unbeliever.

When summer came, Paine moved to back to New Rochelle. He wrote to his friend John Fellows, asking him to come straighten out Paine's financial affairs. Fellows, publisher of the American edition of *The Age of Reason*, arrived in July. He persuaded Paine to sell off sixty acres of his farm for $4,020. Paine was then able to pay off his debts and fix the roof on the cottage.[3]

That winter, Paine spent several weeks with William Carver in New York. Carver was a veterinarian who, in his youth, had cared for Paine's horse in Lewes. Carver showered the old man with attention and care, usually heating a brick for him to warm his bed each night. One night, Paine did it himself and got it too hot. Soon after he went to sleep, the cloth he had wrapped it in burst into flames. Carver broke down the door and rescued him.[4]

In January 1806, Paine wrote to Jefferson to see if the president could get him a pension for his Revolutionary War service. Jefferson ignored the

A Disgruntled Hired Man

Paine had hired Christopher Derrick to help with the work on the farm, but Derrick proved to be lazy and sullen, so Paine fired him. On Christmas Eve, Derrick borrowed a gun, got drunk, and tried to shoot Paine through the window of the cottage. Luckily for Paine, the bullet missed him, although it did go through the wall below the window. Paine did not press charges.

request. Paine became depressed and hardly ate or bathed.

In early spring, Carver went to New Rochelle to visit. He found Paine in terrible condition. Paine was drunk, his clothes were soiled, and he had a ragged beard. Carver said he had to wash him three times with soap and water in order to get him clean. He cut his toenails, which looked like bird claws, shaved him, and cut his hair.

Carver took Paine back to New York City to live with him and his wife. Paine spent his time reading, napping, and writing. He still enjoyed his afternoon walk. He published an essay on the cause of yellow fever (an infectious tropical disease), which was well received, even by his enemies.

On July 25, Paine suffered a stroke. "The fit took me on the stairs, as suddenly as if I had been shot through the head," he recalled.[5] He fell backward down the stairs, landing in a heap on the floor, badly bruised and unconscious. Three weeks later, he said his "mental faculties have remained as perfect as I ever enjoyed them" but he had been hurt so badly by the fall "that I have not been able to get in and out of bed since that day, otherwise than being lifted out in a blanket, by two persons."[6]

Mrs. Carver arranged for Elihu Palmer's widow to care for him. Mrs. Palmer took excellent care of him. However, she began coming less often when she was never paid. In the fall, Paine began complaining. He said that the Carvers left him unattended, served him cold coffee and tea, and refused to build a fire to warm him.

In November, he was able to travel by stagecoach to New Rochelle to vote in the state and congressional elections. However, the supervisor of the election refused to allow him to vote, saying he was not an American citizen. Paine was crushed. Madame Bonneville later said he sued the Board of Inspectors, who were in charge of the election, and lost.

Soon after, William Carver demanded that Paine move out, presenting him with a bill for room and board for twenty-two weeks, as well as for Mrs. Palmer's services. Paine refused, since he had been invited as a guest. Carver even accused him of being the father of Madame Bonneville's boys, although there was no evidence. Finally, John Fellows paid the bill for him.

Paine moved in with John Wesley Jarvis, a sculptor and artist who had painted a flattering portrait of him the year before. Jarvis was only twenty-six, but said the sixty-nine-year-old Paine was "one of the most pleasant companions I have met with for an old man."[7]

Old Friends and Bad Times

Paine renewed his acquaintance with Robert Fulton, who was building a steamboat on the Hudson River. He also published an *Essay on Dreams*, which examined Bible passages based on dreams.

In the spring of 1807, he had a falling-out with James Cheetham, editor of *The American Citizen*. Paine had written many articles for him, but Cheetham edited one of Paine's articles before publishing it. This upset Paine. Paine said he never let anyone change the wording in his writings.

Because Jarvis's busy social life left Paine alone most evenings, he moved in with the family of Zakarias Hitt, a baker who lived on the outskirts of the city. He liked the accommodations but was lonely. Few of his friends journeyed out to see him, and he received little mail.

Early in 1808, Hitt raised the rent from five dollars to seven dollars a week. Saying he could not afford it, Paine moved into a tiny room above a tavern. He appealed in desperation to Congress, asking to be reimbursed for the trip to France with John Laurens back in 1781. Congress refused.

Paine decided to sell part of the New Rochelle farm and found a buyer who would pay $10,000. Unfortunately, soon after the contract was signed, the buyer died. Paine, out of compassion for the widow, released her from the contract.[8]

Friends who visited him that summer of 1808 were appalled at his living conditions. In July, some friends, probably Thomas Emmet and Walter Morton, arranged accommodations for him with Mr. and Mrs. Cornelius Ryder in Greenwich, then a village about a mile and a half north of the city. They bundled him and his belongings into a carriage and whisked him away in his nightshirt to his new home. He had a room on the ground floor, and Mrs. Ryder served him several hot meals each day. Selling the Bordentown house provided rent money.[9]

By now he had little appetite, and no strength in his legs. Cornelius Ryder had to carry him to and from the bed several times a day. He spent most of his time sitting at a table covered with papers and books. He read and dozed most of the time. Ryder said he often found Paine in tears. At these times, he said, the old man was quickly cheered by a little conversation, a smile, or a pat on the shoulder.[10]

Just before Christmas, Paine made his final will. He left money to Mrs. Palmer; Walter Morton, who ran the Phoenix Insurance Company; and Emmet, as well as Clio Rickman and Nicolas de Bonneville, who still had not been allowed to leave France.

His shares in the New York Phoenix Insurance Company (he had paid $1,470 and they were now worth $1,500), his personal effects, and any money he had at the time of his death would go to Madame Bonneville. She was to use the money from the sale of the southern section of the farm to bring up and educate her sons, Thomas and Benjamin. Her oldest son, Louis, had returned to Paris to live with his father.

Paine also requested that he be buried in the Quaker burial ground. He ended his will by stating, "I die in perfect composure and resignation to the will of my Creator, God."[11]

Willett Hicks, a Quaker neighbor, carried Paine's burial request to his fellow members. It was refused. They said his friends and sympathizers "might wish to raise a monument to his memory," which was against their rules. Paine sobbed uncontrollably when he heard the news.[12]

The next day, Madame Bonneville told him she would arrange for him to be buried on the farm. "I have no objection to that," he said. "The farm will be sold and they will dig my bones up before they be half rotten."[13]

Death of the Patriot

Paine grew weaker and his arms and legs began to swell. He lost his appetite and had frequent seizures. He begged Madame Bonneville to move to Greenwich to be with him. She rented rooms nearby, and he was carried there in an armchair on May 4, 1809. Paine was in agony now from bedsores that would not heal. He drifted in and out of consciousness, often crying out in pain.

On the evening of June 7, Dr. James Manley, who was caring for him, asked slowly and deliberately, "Mr. Paine, allow me to ask again. . . . Do you wish to believe that Jesus Christ is the Son of God?"

Paine responded softly, "I have no wish to believe on that subject."[14] Those were his last words. He fell asleep. About 9:00 the next morning, he died.

On June 9, a procession consisting of Madame Bonneville, her son Benjamin, Willett Hicks and two unidentified African Americans made its way with Paine's body the twenty miles to New Rochelle. Emmet and Morton may have gone, too. Some passersby gathered at the grave. Madame Bonneville stood at one end of the grave, positioning Benjamin at the other end. "Oh! Mr. Paine!" she said. "My son stands here as testimony of the gratitude of America, and I, for France."[15]

12

LEGACY

Thomas Paine's greatest gift was his ability to influence others through the written word. His writing helped shape political thinking in three countries: the United States, England, and France.

Paine's work in the United States was most successful, as far as changing opinion and bringing about desired change. *Common Sense* helped the Founding Fathers to unite and finally decide to declare independence from Great Britain. The *Crisis* papers kept up morale in the armed forces and inspired the people to support the fight for independence.

France considered Paine a hero, but the outcome of the French Revolution was not what he had hoped for. He had envisioned a democracy like that of the

United States. He was disappointed when the Constitution did not give everyone the right to vote and when the revolution became violent.

England was certainly the least appreciative of Paine's efforts. He had no success in getting rid of the monarchy. In fact, two hundred years after he tried to convert England to a republic, the monarchy was still firmly in place. However, England is now a constitutional monarchy. The legislature and prime minister have actual political power, while the king or queen is mainly a ceremonial figure.

During most of his life, and for many years after he died, Thomas Paine was a controversial figure. People either loved or hated him; no one was indifferent to him. Only in recent years have Paine's accomplishments come to be understood and appreciated.

Much of the animosity toward Paine can be traced to a few people who were determined to turn public opinion against him. Chalmers's biography and William Pitt's campaign to ruin his reputation with the English people took their toll in England. James Cheetham's biography, published in the United States soon after Paine's death, did much to perpetuate the myths about him in this country. Recently, people have begun to look more objectively at his life and accomplishments.

Paine was considered a drunkard, but that view was denied by many who knew him well. Staple, the clerk who cared for him during his illness in New Rochelle, said he found Paine "really abstemious [refraining from drinking], and when pressed to drink by those on whom he had called . . . he usually refused with great firmness but politely."[1] John Wesley Jarvis, who shared his home with Paine, insisted he was not a drunkard.[2] Soon after Paine returned to America, a newspaper reported, "Mr. Paine is not now, whatever he might have been, inclined to inebriety [drunkenness], but is as abstemious as the tories [loyalists] would wish him otherwise."[3]

Many people also believed Paine was an atheist. This was far from the truth. Although he did not believe in organized religion, he had a deep belief in God. The *Philadelphia Aurora* defended him, saying, "We assert . . . that the writing of that book [*The Age of Reason*], is not a proof of his impiety [lack of respect for God]."[4]

Paine had his faults. He was a little too impressed with his own work, which led to charges that he was conceited. He was proud of his writing and tended

Paine's Statement on Religion to Samuel Adams

Do we want to contemplate His power? We see it in the immensity of creation. Do we want to contemplate His wisdom? We see it in the unchangeable order by which the incomprehensible whole is governed. Do we want to contemplate his munificence [generosity]? We see it in the abundance with which He fills the earth. Do we want to contemplate His mercy? We see it in His not withholding that abundance even from the unthankful.[5]

Today, the Paine Memorial Building stands in New Rochelle, New York. It commemorates the life and work of the patriot who helped inspire Americans during the Revolutionary War.

to talk about it too much. He was not polished and well-dressed; but he was a representative of the common people and he never lost touch with them.

Paine not only wrote about social and political change, but he also acted to bring about change. He wrote *Common Sense* and the *Crisis* papers, and he served in the American Revolution. He did not just write about changes in France, but he also served in the legislature and helped write the constitution.

His unselfishness was commendable. Many of the profits of his writing were donated to worthy causes. He seldom kept more money for himself than he absolutely needed. Paine was always for the underdog and worked long and hard to improve conditions for people from all walks of life. He stood up for the poor, the enslaved, women, and children.

Thomas Paine never lost sight of these goals. He summed up his life in his will: "I have lived an honest and useful life to mankind; my time has been spent in doing good."[6]

CHRONOLOGY

1737—Born on January 29 in Thetford, England.

1750—Becomes an apprentice in his father's staymaker's shop.

1756—Serves on the British privateer *King of Prussia*.

1759—*September 27*: Marries Mary Lambert, who dies the next year.

1762—Enters the excise service.

1771—*March 26*: Marries Elizabeth Ollive.

1772—Writes *Case of the Officers of the Excise*.

1773—Separates from his wife, Elizabeth.

1774—*November 30*: Arrives in America.

1776—*Common Sense* is published; The Declaration of Independence is signed; The first *Crisis* paper is published.

1777 —Serves as secretary to the committee for foreign
–1779   affairs.

1777 —Twelve more *Crisis* papers appear.
–1783

1781—Goes to France with John Laurens to negotiate for money and supplies.

1785 —Designs an iron bridge.
–1787

1787—Goes to Europe to try to sell his bridge.

1791—Part I of *Rights of Man* is published in England.

1792—Part II of *Rights of Man* is published; Receives summons to trial; Flees from England to France; Takes a seat in French National Convention; Convicted of seditious libel in England while he is in France.

1793—*December 28*: Is imprisoned at the Luxembourg.

1794—*November 4*: Is released from prison; Part I of *The Age of Reason* appears.

1796—Writes *Letter to George Washington*.

1802—*October 30*: Arrives back in the United States.

1803
–1809—Moves back and forth from Bordentown to New York to New Rochelle.

1809—Dies on June 8 in New York City.

CHAPTER NOTES

Chapter 1. Inspiration in a Crisis

1. John Keane, *Tom Paine: A Political Life* (Boston: Little, Brown and Company, 1995), p. 140.

2. David Powell, *Tom Paine: The Greatest Exile* (New York: St. Martin's Press, 1985), p. 89.

3. Jack Fruchtman, Jr., *Thomas Paine: Apostle of Freedom* (New York: Four Walls Eight Windows, 1994), p. 90.

4. Thomas Paine, "The American Crisis," *Pennsylvania Journal and the Weekly Advertiser*, December 1, 1776.

5. Ibid.

6. Ibid.

7. Eric Foner, "Thomas Paine," *The World Book Multimedia Encyclopedia* (Chicago: World Book, Inc., 1996).

Chapter 2. Growing Up in Thetford

1. John Keane, *Tom Paine: A Political Life* (Boston: Little, Brown and Company, 1995), p. 16.

2. Mary Agnes Best, *Thomas Paine, Prophet and Martyr of Democracy* (New York: Harcourt, Brace & Company, 1927), p. 7.

3. David Freeman Hawke, *Paine* (New York: Harper & Row Publishers, 1974), p. 9.

4. David Powell, *Tom Paine: The Greatest Exile* (New York: St. Martin's Press, 1985), p. 13.

5. Hawke, p. 9.

6. Olivia Coolidge, *Tom Paine, Revolutionary* (New York: Charles Scribner's Sons, 1969), p. 4.

7. Jerome D. Wilson and William E. Ricketson, *Thomas Paine* (Boston: Twayne Publishers, 1989), p. 3.

8. Keane, p. 38.

Chapter 3. Two Jobs and a Marriage

1. John Keane, *Tom Paine: A Political Life* (Boston: Little, Brown and Company, 1995), p. 45.

2. Ibid., p. 46.

3. David Freeman Hawke, *Paine* (New York: Harper & Row Publishers, 1974), p. 11.

Chapter 4. Disillusioned With England

1. John Keane, *Tom Paine: A Political Life* (Boston: Little, Brown and Company, 1995), p. 59.

2. Ibid., p. 60.

3. Olivia Coolidge, *Tom Paine, Revolutionary* (New York: Charles Scribner's Sons, 1969), p. 11.

4. Keane, p. 66.

5. Ibid., p. 69.

6. David Powell, *Tom Paine: The Greatest Exile* (New York: St. Martin's Press, 1985), p. 46.

7. David Freeman Hawke, *Paine* (New York: Harper & Row Publishers, 1974), p. 18.

8. Ibid., p. 20.

9. Jerome D. Wilson and William E. Ricketson, *Thomas Paine* (Boston: Twayne Publishers, 1989), p. 7.

10. Keane, p. 78.

11. Ibid.

Chapter 5. *Common Sense*

1. David Freeman Hawke, *Paine* (New York: Harper & Row Publishers, 1974), p. 25.

2. John Keane, *Tom Paine: A Political Life* (Boston: Little, Brown and Company, 1995), p. 92.

3. Ibid., p. 100.

4. Ibid., p. 95.

5. Frank Smith, *Thomas Paine, Liberator* (New York: Frederick A. Stokes, 1938), p. 17.

6. David Powell, *Tom Paine: The Greatest Exile* (New York: St. Martin's Press, 1985), p. 62.

7. Smith, p. 19.

8. Hawke, p. 37.

9. Smith, p. 18.

10. Keane, p. 101.

11. Powell, p. 70.

12. Olivia Coolidge, *Tom Paine, Revolutionary* (New York: Charles Scribner's Sons, 1969), p. 34.

13. Ibid.

14. Powell, p. 73.

Chapter 6. *Crisis* Papers and Silas Deane

1. Jack Fruchtman, Jr., *Thomas Paine: Apostle of Freedom* (New York: Four Walls Eight Windows, 1994), p. 94.

2. Jerome D. Wilson and William E. Ricketson, *Thomas Paine* (Boston: Twayne Publishers, 1989), p. 31.

3. John Keane, *Tom Paine: A Political Life* (Boston: Little, Brown and Company, 1995), p. 155.

4. Wilson & Ricketson, p. 32.

5. Keane, p. 167.

6. Ibid., pp. 173–174.

7. David Freeman Hawke, *Paine* (New York: Harper & Row Publishers, 1974), p. 87.

Chapter 7. A Trip Abroad and the End of the War

1. Olivia Coolidge, *Tom Paine, Revolutionary* (New York: Charles Scribner's Sons, 1969), p. 70.

2. John Keane, *Tom Paine: A Political Life* (Boston: Little, Brown and Company, 1995), pp. 206–207.

3. Jack Fruchtman, Jr., *Thomas Paine: Apostle of Freedom* (New York: Four Walls Eight Windows, 1994), p. 133.

4. Keane, p. 211.

5. Ibid., p. 216.

6. Ibid., p. 234.

7. Ibid.

8. Ibid., p. 235.

9. Coolidge, p. 76.

10. Internet Infidels, "The American Crisis No. XIII," *Thomas Paine*, March 17, 2000, <http://libertyonline.hypermall.com/Paine/Crisis/Crisis-TOC.html> (May 30, 2000).

11. Keane, p. 247.

12. Ibid.

13. Ibid., p. 252.

14. Ibid., p. 253.

Chapter 8. Bridging the Gap Between America and Europe

1. Jack Fruchtman, Jr., *Thomas Paine: Apostle of Freedom* (New York: Four Walls Eight Windows, 1994), p. 163.

2. Jerome D. Wilson and William E. Ricketson, *Thomas Paine* (Boston: Twayne Publishers, 1989), p. 47.

3. Fruchtman, p. 185.

4. John Keane, *Tom Paine: A Political Life* (Boston: Little, Brown and Company, 1995), pp. 285–286.

5. Fruchtman, p. 192.

6. Ibid., p. 194.

7. Ibid., p. 193.

Chapter 9. England and France Turn Against Paine

1. John Keane, *Tom Paine: A Political Life* (Boston: Little, Brown and Company, 1995), p. 294.

2. Ibid., p. 295.

3. Ibid., p. 307.

4. David Powell, *Tom Paine: The Greatest Exile* (New York: St. Martin's Press, 1985), p. 189.

5. Ibid., p. 194.

6. Keane, p. 314.

7. Ibid., p. 317.

8. Powell, p. 206.

9. Ibid., p. 210.

10. Keane, p. 343.

11. Ibid., p. 348.

12. Lou Gurko, *Tom Paine: Freedom's Apostle* (New York: Thomas Y. Crowell Company, 1957), p. 159.

13. Ibid., pp. 160–161.

14. Ibid., p. 153.

Chapter 10. Better Times in France

1. Olivia Coolidge, *Tom Paine, Revolutionary* (New York: Charles Scribner's Sons, 1969), p. 155.

2. John Keane, *Tom Paine: A Political Life* (Boston: Little, Brown and Company, 1995), p. 418.

3. Ibid., p. 419.

4. David Freeman Hawke, *Paine* (New York: Harper & Row Publishers, 1974, p. 307.

5. Ibid., p. 311.

6. Jack Fruchtman, Jr., *Thomas Paine: Apostle of Freedom* (New York: Four Walls Eight Windows, 1994), p. 350.

7. David Powell, *Tom Paine: The Greatest Exile* (New York: St. Martin's Press, 1985), p. 252.

8. Hawke, p. 324.

9. S. M. Berthold, *Thomas Paine: America's First Liberal* (Boston: Meador Publishing Company, 1938), p. 198.

10. Keane, p. 444.

11. Hawke, p. 338.

12. Keane, p. 457.

Chapter 11. Later Years in America

1. John Keane, *Tom Paine: A Political Life* (Boston: Little, Brown and Company, 1995), p. 467.

2. Ibid.

3. Ibid., p. 504.

4. Ibid., p. 507.

5. Ibid., p. 517.

6. Ibid.

7. Olivia Coolidge, *Tom Paine, Revolutionary* (New York: Charles Scribner's Sons, 1969), p. 195.

8. Keane, p. 529.

9. Ibid., p. 531.

10. Ibid.

11. Ibid., p. 533.

12. Ibid., p. 534.

13. Coolidge, p. 201.

14. Ibid.

15. Fruchtman, p. 433.

Chapter 12. Legacy

1. John Keane, *Tom Paine: A Political Life* (Boston: Little, Brown and Company, 1995), p. 493.

2. David Freeman Hawke, *Paine* (New York: Harper & Row Publishers, 1974), p. 389.

3. Ibid., p. 356.

4. Keane, p. 459.

5. Ibid., p. 476.

6. Ibid., p. 533.

GLOSSARY

aide-de-camp—An assistant to an army officer.

Anglican Church—The official church in England during Paine's childhood.

atheist—A person who does not believe in God.

Bastille—A prison in Paris in the late 1700s.

Continental Congress—A group of representatives from all the American colonies that met as a governing body throughout the American Revolution.

effigy—A dummy representing a hated person.

excise officers—People employed in England to collect taxes.

Federalists—Members of a political group, led by Alexander Hamilton and John Adams, who believed in a strong central government.

Girondins—Members of a French political party from 1791–1793, who advocated slow and orderly change of government.

Hessians—German soldiers hired to fight for the British during the American Revolution.

Jacobins—Members of a French political party during the French Revolution. They had radical beliefs and were behind most of the executions of Girondins and others.

Louisiana Purchase—Large area of land bought from France in 1803 for $15 million. It extended from the Mississippi River to the Rocky Mountains and from the Gulf of Mexico to Canada.

monarchy—Form of government headed by a king or queen.

Parliament—The British lawmaking body.

patriots—Colonists who supported the American Revolution.

Quakers—Members of the Society of Friends, a peaceful religious group.

republic—A nation in which the power rests with representatives elected by the people.

Royalist—A person whose sympathy is with the monarchy.

FURTHER READING

Books

Farley, Karin C. *Thomas Paine*. Austin, Tex.: Raintree Steck-Vaughn Publishers, 1992.

Fisher, Bruce. *Thomas Paine*. New York: Chelsea House Publishers, 1999.

Keane, John. *Tom Paine: A Political Life*. Boston: Little, Brown and Company, 1995.

Kent, Deborah. *The American Revolution: "Give Me Liberty, or Give Me Death!"* Hillside, N.J.: Enslow Publishers, Inc., 1994.

Meltzer, Milton. *Tom Paine: Voice of Revolution*. Danbury, Conn.: Franklin Watts, Inc., 1996.

McGowen, Tom. *Robespierre and the French Revolution in World History*. Berkeley Heights, N.J.: Enslow Publishers, Inc., 2000.

Vail, John. *Thomas Paine*. New York: Chelsea House Publishers, 1990.

Internet Addresses

PBS Online. "The Remains of Thomas Paine." *Liberty!* 1997. <http://www.pbs.org/ktca/liberty/chronicle/paine.html>.

Thomas Paine National Historical Association. n.d. <http://www.thomas-paine.com>.

INDEX